Brother Love Runs Deep

In These San Jose Streets

Based On A True Story

HOPPER

PAGE PUBLISHING
Conneaut Lake, PA

First originally published by Page Publishing 2023

ISBN 979-8-88654-924-9 (pbk)
ISBN 979-8-88654-926-3 (hc)
ISBN 979-8-88654-925-6 (digital)

Printed in the United States of America

First of all, I would like to thank our precious Lord.

Then my beloved mom and dad; baby sister, Jackie; and myself for taking the time to write this story. All my strength to put into words the good and bad mistakes. Maybe those who read this book can learn from me. Much love and God bless all of you people always. Amen. And my high school teacher Mrs. Dunn for teaching me how to write my feelings into words.

Now I'm fifty-three and wish I made better choices, but I did have fun and tears all my years. Amen. We smile now and cry later.

CONTENTS

Chapter 1: My Early Years...1

Chapter 2: Moving in with My Tio (Uncle), the Connection.....14

Chapter 3: Going to San Jose Jailhouse..33

Chapter 4: Not Learning My Lesson, Going to Prison 44

Chapter 5: Back on the San Jose Streets Again 62

Chapter 6: Going Back to Prison, San Quentin 72

Chapter 7: Getting Out of Prison, Close Call Getting Shot At...82

Chapter 8: Out and About after a Year of Lockup......................97

Chapter 9: Mine and Gordy's First Daughter, Destiny 118

Chapter 10: Just Finished Doing One Hundred Days
and Nights Locked Up 131

Chapter 11: Getting Caught Up in LA Jailhouse.......................151

CHAPTER 1

MY EARLY YEARS

I was born in April 1963. My name is William Christopher Shake. What kind of name is that? My dad is half Italian and half German. My mother is full-blooded Latina. When I was in school, the other kids would begin to tease me about my last name—like shake and bake. I would ask them after a while if they wanted to fight after school. Most of the time, they said no, so I would just go to my classes with no trouble.

Once in the third grade, I had a crush on this one little female; her name was Ann Marie. I think that she had a little crush on me too. This one day after our class was over, she got tripped by this other guy. Then I told him to stop it or we would have to fight after school. He said, "Sure, I will fight after school." So it was on after school. There was a big statue right in front of the school. We went to Anne Darling Elementary School, right on Thirty-Third Street and McKee, very busy part of town. So I waited for this guy near the statue. Here he came; we squared off. There were a lot of other classmates there, waiting for us to get them up. The bell rang. "Let's begin." We danced around for just a minute. Then I cracked him in the mouth, then I hit him again till he started to cry—cool.

This guy had two older brothers who were watching us, so his fourth-grade brother wanted to fight with me too. I was just a little scared, but I said, "You want some too?" We began to start fighting, and I landed a good punch to his face then hit him again till he started to cry—cool. What would you know, he had one more brother in the fifth grade who wanted to fight me too. I guess I got Aztec fire in my blood; I said, "You want some of me too? Come on then." Then we began to fight. I danced around him, waiting for an opening, then laid one on him too—*crack, crack*—till he started to cry and said he had enough. Whoa, everything had happened so fast. I just heard the crowd cheering me on. "You're a bad dude, William. We want to hang around with you." I said, "I fight for the honor and respect—that about it." Hey, I patted myself on the back for that. Ms. Ann Marie was watching too. She was happy that I did not get hurt and thanked me for defending her honor.

They sent me to live with my mother in the fourth grade. She lived with her new boyfriend and my little brother and little sister, plus my new half-brother. My mother lived in a duplex that she rented from her uncle who lived next door from us. It was on the westside of town, Bird and Virginia. We went to Gardner Elementary School, walking distance from the house. I started to make new friends, playing four square before class. Then one day after school, while I was walking home with some friends and my girl cousin, Arlene, this one guy passed us sticking the finger at me and Arlene. So I said to the friends I was with that I would like to fight with that guy. Then they told him what I said. The next day after school, I got home and helped my mother with the dishes. I heard some knocking on the front door; I got the door. Guess who? One of his friends told me to come outside. There I went. Next door, there was a crowd of his friends, plus Mr. Finger. "*What's up?* I heard that you wanna fight me. Sure, let's get busy." We started to dance around for a minute. Then I rushed to him and took him to the ground and started cracking him again and again till he gave up. I let him up and told him not to be flipping off me or my people—cool. So everybody knew that I would and could fight and that I was not a big crybaby. I would only fight out of honor and respect for my little sister and brother.

While we were at school one day, someone broke into our house; I'd seen all kinds of cops around making the report. They stole my little piggy bank plus some other stuff. My new stepfather said, "What can you do? Just be thankful that nobody got hurt or nothing." I guess he did not want me around.

I lived with my auntie (*tia*) when I was young. I did things that most young boys would do. One day—I was about ten years old—I was playing in the backyard. Oh man, this yard was huge. So I went to the farthest part; near the fence, there was long dry grass. I had some matches and started little fires then stomped them out. Then I started another one—what a rush for me. This one just got away from me, and I *panicked*. I ran inside the house, pretending to be the stupid one. My uncle Johnny was home and said, "What's that popping noise?"

"I think that might be the fire that I lit."

Then my uncle thought fast, got the water hose, and dragged it to the fire. In about one minute, it was out. He said, "What are you trying to do, light the whole block on fire?"

I said, "No. I'm sorry, Tio. Thank you."

"Let us keep our mouths shut."

"No problem."

There was an old footstool back there too, so we ripped it open. The inside had like dry grass—too good to be true, good cover-up. So everything went fine for about two weeks, then my older tio Chico gave me up and snitched me out. When I went to show my other tio Tony from marriage, he said, "Where's the fire, mijo? I don't see nothing."

"Look at the fence."

"Now I can see the burnt marks."

First, I got a spanking from my tia then spent two weeks in my room, straight home after school. "No fun for you, mister." Hey, I had it all coming; that was just all in the game. Then I was done playing with matches, that's for sure.

A month after that, I had to move in with my father; my dad was mean and strict with me. Me being the oldest, I had to be good and be an example to my little sister and brother. So all that I could do was make the best of my situation, *que no*? Then it was not so bad, just got a little lonely once in a while. My father had remarried, so I had a stepmother who had two children also, a boy my age plus a girl who was my sister's age. We all got along together the best possible way, I guess. We would go swim at Ryland Park. I got my little bike stolen at that sweet park. I still went to visit my grandma on some weekends, kicked it real hard with my tios, and ride our bikes all up and down.

So now I was living with my father and his new wife. Her name was Lupe; she had two kids of her own. Her son was about my age; Andrew was his name. Then he had a little sister; her name was Yolanda. I would try and make the best of it. We would ride our bikes around the block. I started to notice that my new stepbrother would get into his own trouble with my father. So my father would make sure that Andrew did not get away with anything. My dad gave Andrew his due punishment always—grounded him, spanked him. Hey, it's not easy to be a stepfather; I know now that I'm older. You always treat your kids better than your stepkids—not because you want to but just because blood is thicker than water. My father was harder on Andrew than he was with me.

This one morning, I asked Andrew for my mother's telephone number. Then he told me that his mother said not to give it to me. I got angry and started a fight with my stepbrother till he started to cry. He finally gave up my mother's phone number. So I called my mother, telling her that I didn't like living with my father; I was crying, wiping my little tears. My mother comforted me and told me that everything would be all right; that helped me. The very next day, I heard knocking on the door. It was all Andrew's friends, asking me why I beat up Andrew, so I told them why. Then we started to talk, and they wanted to be my friends, and we were cool. My father was not too happy and ended up splitting up with his new wife.

So I was now living at my grandmother's house—just like my mother had told me that everything was going to be all right. My grandmother lived on Ninth and Empire, so I had to transfer to a new school, Grant Elementary School. I was in fifth grade. I got to my first class. I started to check out the new females who would be around me. My new classmates did start to tease me about my last name, but that was not so bad. Then I started making new friends. Then my uncle went there too. He did not make fun of me; that was cool. After school, we would hang out and chill out and talk to the females. I was talking to this one female; her name was Rosemary, very pretty, a star. We would start to get our little make out on. This was after school; we would meet up and make out on the benches. She made me feel like a young Aztec warrior; she was an Azteca princess. Me being the new boy in school, I was like fresh meat for the females—in a good way. I really did get attached to Ms. Rosemary; I thought that she felt the same about me too. I was so wrong; she broke up with me for nothing and left me crying all alone. Right at school, I cried, trying to hold back my little tears. My friends would try and comfort me. "What's the matter?" All that I could say was "Why did she break my heart?" wiping my tears away. Trying to hold my head up, I stayed strong till I'd meet someone new to share some company. My father had found an apartment, so we moved from my grandmother's house, just my dad and me.

I would just get a little lonely with my father at the apartment. My dad lived on Fourth and San Fernando, right across the street from San José State University. I would still go visit my grandmother's house on the weekends. I would ride my little bike down Santa Clara Street till I got to Ninth Street, and I was at my grandmother's house. Sometimes my dad would let me spend the night. So this one night, while I was at my grandmother's house with my two uncles, we decided to break into this elementary school, Horace Mann. This school was right on Santa Clara and Seventh Street. We broke one window with no alarms and no cops. Then we got two shopping carts waiting. I climbed into the window and saw some typewriters. We started to load them inside the shopping carts then started to make our little getaway back to Grandma's house. Then we sneaked the typewriters inside and started to type out some crazy stuff. First, like William was wanted for murder and bank robbery. Well, one of our friends had a big mouth and gave us up. He had told the school, then they told the cops. We had hidden the typewriters in my uncle's bedroom. It was in the summertime, so we went to San Jose High School to swim. My uncles and I were having a good time. Then all of a sudden, we saw all kinds of cops surrounding the swimming pool. They pulled out me and my uncle Frank and took us away to juvenile hall. Now we were at the juvie hall, little kids who got our cherry busted.

So they took us away, and we weren't even crying. We got to juvenile hall, went through the booking, and got processed to our new clothes. I didn't see my uncle; they sent me to B-12 unit for younger cellmates. What a mess that I got myself into. Weekends was for visiting, so my mother came to visit with a happy meal. That sure did brighten up my weekend. She told me she still loved me and not to be stealing anymore—unless I liked my new home. She was so right; I sure hated to be locked up and could not wait to be released. I told her that I had learned my lesson way too well. Then my father was mad at me too for getting into trouble. While I had to deal with my new home at juvenile hall, I met other young men who got caught, so I made some new friends to pass the time. Some of them were ready to go to the ranch; they could not wait to get there, talking about getting buffed out. I myself just could not wait to get out of there. Then I told myself again that this was not for me. After two weeks, I got released to my father. Me trying to forget all about that place, juvie hall, I put this experience all behind me. When we would get to go outside for baseball and see these other inmates, how healthy and strong they had looked to me—like true Aztec warriors all ready for the battlefield. Hey, now I was free and ready to enjoy this life that I was blessed with. I still had a little summer vacation left, so I might as well make the best of it, *que no*, brother? At least till school started once again.

I stayed out of trouble after that juvenile hall scare—for the most part. Then living with my father was not all that bad. My little brother would come to visit me two weekends a month. We would play near San José State University, which was right across the street. We would play catch with the football or go to Horace Mann to play some basketball. We'd sometimes go to the movies, hang out downtown, and play the pinball machines; we had a blast together. My brother's name was Albert; sometimes we would just hang out at the house and play some music. While our dad went to the bowling alley to have his fun. See, my dad had an oldie collection, so we would listen to the best oldies in town. We would hang out at the Lucky's to help out some people with the grocery bags to earn some money. Then we had a little money to mess around town then go to the Jose Theatre; that was the spot to meet some young females. Hey, see, if we might get lucky, sooner or later, we had to take that chance. Then when we would listen to some of these oldies; my little brother would start to sing—note for note, baby boy. My brother sang some Smokey. When he did his thing, singing, people would stop and listen to him; the young females went wild. He sounded like he would be famous or something then danced like James Brown or Michael Jackson, doing his thing. This was his song: "You Really Got a Hold on Me."

As my little brother, Albert, grew older, he started to polish his singing and dancing skills. When my brother would sing, I would have to stop to listen. My dad was the manager of the apartments on Fourth and San Fernando, so he rented my grandmother a small two-bedroom cottage right behind us—cool. I was happy that my two uncles and my grandmother were right next door. Now my uncle and I had been out of trouble for about two years—lovely. I was about fourteen, chilling out at my grandma's house, when my uncle Frank was ironing his pants and burned them with the iron by mistake. He then decided to wait till midnight and break into this men's store, Art Martinez. Well, this store was right on First Street and San Fernando, real busy with cops. The thing was, there was a chance that we might just get busted, but what the heck, we'd try anyways. So now it was about that magic time, midnight. "Let's get ready and do this caper." We put on dark clothing, then my two uncles and I were good to go. Then we started walking up San Fernando till we got to First, just checking out the area. All looked pretty silent. We waited in the shadows for about ten minutes. Then we went into action; we first broke the big front window and waited about one minute. No alarms—cool. We made our way into the store and started to grab some pants, gangster hats, brims, and then some shirts. We had no time to shop and just got in and out as fast as we could without getting busted. Now it was time to make our little getaway, and we did make it back home.

So now we made it back and started to look through our new clothes. We were happy that nobody got busted, and we were going to keep our mouths shut. We pulled this one off clean. Then in about six months, my grandmother moved back to the eastside of town, near Mayfair Park. My dad really did not like me around my two uncles (*tios*). My dad said that they would lead into that trouble, so then I started to run away from home for weeks a time. He would want me to come home; sometimes, I did come back home just for a while. I would stay at my mother's side of the family, like my grandma's or my aunt's house. My dad would say to me, "You only want to stay at your grandma's to get into trouble." So right he was.

Now my dad would have to pay child support. I told my dad regardless that he would have to pay for my support, food, and shelter, plus new school clothes. So finally, my dad gave in and let me move into my grandma's house. I was still in junior high school, Peter Burnett; this school was on Second and Hedding Street. This was when I first started to sell some marijuana joints for $2 a joint. I kept everything low-key, got my money, and went to my classes. So my weed was for free—just had to sell some to make money to get some more. At that time, you could get one ounce for $60 then break it down into joints. I went to school most of the time; that was where all the business was at. I took all the basics: reading, math, and PE. Everything was going smooth, for the most part, living with my grandmother.

I can remember this one day when out of the blue, my little brother, Albert, called me. Albert told me that this one guy was messing with him, so I told him that I would be right over and to let me get ready and took one of my uncles with me. So we caught the bus to Santa Clara and met my brother at the swimming pool; we started to talk. Then Albert said, "There he is." So I hit him up and told him who I was, Albert's big brother, Chino, from San Jo. All of a sudden, he went into a karate stance. Shit, I froze right there on the spot. I got scared just a little bit.

My uncle said, "What just happened? You got clowned right in front of your little brother."

"Yeah, I know, bro." I told my brother how sorry I was.

So the next day, I went to the boxing gym to learn to box. My brother forgave me and said nothing more about the subject. Now that I was in training, I did feel better about this situation; it only made me train that much harder. About one month later, I went to visit my brother in Santa Clara on the bus. I took my uncle Frank with me, plus we had about five Chevy keys; we said we would steal a Chevy on the way back to San Jo. So our little visit was over, and we were on the hunt for a clean Chevy. We found this one '64 Super Sport, two-door, all original, gold with a white top. It was about ten in the night. We first saw if the key would fit the doors—booyah— unlocked the car, pushed it down the street, got in, and started her up. "Let's get ghosting." We took the backstreets till we hit the El Camino. We passed juvenile hall with our heads low. Yeah, we were young and dumb passing by that juvenile hall. I got this hankie over my head, then we passed this one cop, lucky he must have been getting off his shift.

So now we went to my other uncle's work and showed him this car that we just had stolen. We chilled out there for about one hour, then we left back to the madhouse. I had thought that we could be low-key, showing the other homeboys the clean '64 Chevy. So we were just killing time, then I saw this one lowrider female.

I started to get at her. "What's your name, and what's up with you, baby girl?" So we started to talk; her name was Karen. She was a runaway, and she needed a ride to pick up some of her stuff at her parents' house. I told her that we would take her to her house. It was on White Road and Martin, so off we went till we got to the house. We all went inside and let her get her stuff; we wanted something hard to drink. We found some and took them with us, then we left back to the madhouse. Now Karen felt safe with me, and we started to make out in the back seat. My uncle sat in the front seat, listening to the music. We started taking little shots of that brandy, then we all fell asleep till about five the next morning. It was still a little foggy. We started the car and left down the street, Twenty-Fourth and Bonita. As soon as we hit that first corner, I saw this cop car right behind us. I told my tio, "If we get busted, we are going to the ranch, so let's giddyap." Now this cop (*placa*) turned on his strawberry lights on us; we couldn't turn back.

Now this cop (*placa*) was right on our heels. We turned on San Antonio bridge, went over the freeway, then made the first left turn then one more left turn till we were back on San Antonio Street, going toward King Road. We hit Jackson and made a right-hand turn, going to Story Road, then we made a left-hand turn on Cinderella Street. We needed to get to the catwalk then bust out of the car. My tio hit the next street and made another left turn. He opened his door, trying to get halfway out the car; his knee was scraping the road. He jumped out and ran up the catwalk, then Karen followed him. The cop then grabbed Karen by her hair and held her. I myself opened my door and started to run through some backyards till I hit the freeway (280), ran across, and made it back to my grandma's house. I met my tio there. What a clean getaway. We were looking through the window and saw all kinds of cops (*placas*) looking for us till they finally stopped. I told my tio, "You got that Aztec U-turn for these rookies."

"This is our San Jo town. We do know these streets. We are cool after that grand theft auto. Back to that lowriding, baby boy. I'm so glad that we did not get busted. Time to be good and stay away from that long arm of the law."

"That was raw, cutting them corners, Tio Frank. Booyah."

"Yeah."

Later, an older friend said, "Check this out, Chino. You want an after-school job at the cheese factory?" His name was Manual. "Everything is all set up."

"Sweet."

"You can get work credits for school and have a little work experience and extra money, plus I already got you an interview."

"Cool."

"So be there Friday at 3:00 p.m., and don't forget."

I went to job interview, and they told me my hours were three to five thirty. You start on Monday. Thank you, and have a nice weekend."

I was happy; I got home and told my grandma about my new job. She was happy for me also. "You work hard and do a good job."

"You got it."

It was Friday—time to get my party on. So Smiley and I went to visit our lady friend, Ms. Mary Q, to chill out and get a little drink on.

"Hey, Mary, is it okay for us to chill and drink a couple of brews?"

"Yeah, just don't get wild."

So we started to kick backhand pop open a brew and gave her one. We started to talk about the things on the block.

"Hey, where's your son, Birdy?"

"Oh, he got into some trouble. They sent him away to CYA—that's the California Youth Authority—for twenty-two months."

"That's too bad. Well, I'll see him when he gets out."

Robert, known as Birdy, was sent to Preston; I heard it was like gladiator school. I knew that Birdy had already did time at the Ranch for a while; now he was with some hard-core young warriors. I asked Mary Q why she called her son Birdy. She told me that at the time she was doing her time in jail, she was pregnant with Birdy; he was her little jailbird. "Thanks for sharing that story with us." I felt really bad for my friend; most of his teenage years, he spent behind bars. We'd play, and we'd pay—simple rules. Then I told her, "Next time you visit Birdy, send him my love and the utmost respect."

"Will do."

"Well, it's time to get back to my grandma's house. See you later, Mary Q."

See, about six months earlier, when I was visiting her house, she got almost robbed by some dope fiends. I just happened to be there at the time. First, I heard banging on the front door, then I looked at Mary Q. She said, "Don't let them inside," so I didn't. I was looking through the front glass window and saw a gun.

"Open up the door."

"No, no, don't, mijo."

I stayed by her side, while others ran out back door.

They finally entered the house and asked Mary Q, "Where's the drugs?"

"Ain't got none. Take whatever, please."

"Please don't hurt us," I said, standing right in front of the man with the gun. We heard the SJPD coming, so the bad guys tried to make a fast getaway. They busted all three of them. Whoa, that was like a movie or something. It all happened so fast, unreal, but it was way too real. Then Mary Q gave me a long hug and said, "You are like an Aztec warrior, fearless, would have taken a bullet for me. That's gangsta. I don't even trip." She loved me just like one of her own. Well, just another day in the life that we were blessed with.

We—my tio Smiley and I—got back to his mom's house and drank and smoked.

"What a crazy life that I lead."

"It's all part of the game, baby boy."

So my two tios and I were just like bros. We shared the chores around the house, also used one another's clothes, and listened to the best gangsta oldies in the SJ town that we called home.

So I was getting ready to start my new job at the cheese factory. I got there ten minutes early; they got me landscaping the grounds. I got my tools and began to make the place look better little by little. Then on breaks, I talked to the other crew members—some I did know, others I did not know. One day, here came none other Mr. Joesoph Bonanno with two of his henchmen. I just looked up, and there he was, just checking the grounds, plus other things. These men where big Italian you didn't wanna mess with. That was if you knew the truth about what could take place or just the trouble you might find yourself in. I never looked twice or locked eyes with any of them. I would guess out of pure respect. I saw the Bonanno Storyd in 2008. His father had lost his brother when he was young himself. Then his father wanted peace and had the family they were at war with baptize Joe Bonanno; he was the dove of love to bring peace for both families. That was why they called that move the peacemaker. We live in this crazy world; you do what you must just to survive, *que no?* One time, Mr. Bonanno gave me a wave. "Good job."

"Thank you, Mr. Bonanno."

Everything was going fine at my grandma's house; I was going to school and chilling with all the lowrider dudes. I mean, it was like a new style of acting and dressing. They were hard-core dudes, *vatos*, who had their. I liked the feeling, so little by little, I started to change my ways and got a baldy haircut. So I could be like them; they looked cool to me. The girls really liked this new lowrider image, I must say. This style started when some heads went to LA to visit their southern part of the family. They would say, "They hard-core low-rider over there doing it, gangbanging, and throwing up their block, hoods, sets, and the barrios. Where you from, and who do you represent? What do you represent?" It sounded good to a lot of us being young at that time. I never joined any of those gangs myself; I was just trying to stay away from that stuff. So I was helping around my grandma's house, watering the backyard; she planted squash and some tomatoes—let's not forget the chilies. My grandma would use all vegetables that we planted for dinner and breakfast. Chilies just off the vine—tell me how fresh was that. I was still doing my light-weight dealing just to make that extra money and have some weed, so sometimes I would go visit my older cousin (*primo*) to get some more marijuana. He had all the good stuff plus was safer for me; he was family. Then he would have to leave and leave me in charge of the fort. One day, he said, "How would you like to live with me, mijo?"

"Well, let me think about it first."

He talked to my grandma to see how she felt; whatever I wanted to do was okay. See, my grandma was poor and was just making it. Then I said to myself, "What the heck, and if it doesn't work out, the door would always be open at my grandma's house." She gave me her blessing.

Chapter 2

Moving in with My Tio (Uncle), the Connection

So I packed my stuff and moved in with Robert, the connection. I was going to make some money. He lived in Meadowfair; that was the eastside by Eastridge, Kind Road, and Tully Road. Robert ran the block and always had drugs for sale. He sold marijuana plus heroin. I started to feel the power that he carried. Like a big-time gangster or small Mafia, he would introduce me as his son. "Chino is with me," untouchable or something. Hey, I did like all the power and utmost respect toward me. I did not let this get to my head. I Just did what the boss said, followed my orders, and didn't ask questions. He was good to me and got me back in school; that was great. Yeah, this program was cool with me. I went to school, got back home, and broke down the marijuana into ounces, halves, quarters, then some twenties.

This one day after school, I got home. I told Robert that I wanted to start to box once again. He gave me $100 to get my gear, like a heavy punching bag, then whatever I needed to start. I was about fifteen at this time, on top of the world. I was going to San José High School, where I wanted to learn and be a better person. I always went to school, had my lunch money, and chilled out with my homeboys.

So at lunchtime, I'd go get something to eat off campus then check out all the hot-looking females who might give us some action.

I would go to the park on Santa Clara, Roosevelt; they had a center there where everyone would hang out at—all the lowriders' young warriors and the Azteca princesses.

This was when that street gang stuff took off; we had two main gangs. I did not like it myself, but what could you do? So we had lomas locos, then we had norte homeboys. We had all went to the same school. I knew the homeboys from both sides; I would stay out of their business. I just went to my boxing training to protect my little brother and sister, plus myself. Like a true Aztec warrior, I walked all alone and fought all alone with no backup. Going to school was cool; I got to see all the young pretty females and see if I might get lucky.

Then at school, talking to them and walking them to class was showing respect. We all would look at the lowriders pass the school on lunch breaks and get some new ideas for when we got our own lowriders.

After school, we would go chill out at the Roosevelt center, play pool, or talk to the pretty females. One day, I spotted this one fine-looking chica who was all alone, so I went and started to get at her. "Hey, what's your name? And you look so pretty." She told me her name was Martha. "My name is William, but they do call me Chino." We started to talk. "How you doing?"

"All right."

I told her that I trained at the gym to box.

She said, "Cool, now you can protect me, if someone was messing with me." Martha told me that they called her Chica.

"That's cool."

We hit it off right out of the gate. After one week, Chica gave me her phone number so we could keep in touch; so little by little, I just might have her in my arms. Well, I could not get my hopes up with Chica, just see what might happen. So I would stay busy doing my own program, dealing and making money after class.

I had a pretty full day—going to school, going to boxing, and to top it off, taking care of business at the home front. I was waiting for customers who were looking for that marijuana, then you got $50 then the small twenties, so everything was running smooth with this cool program. I would do this till about nine, and my shift was over. What along day, then I do it all over again. Life was good for me overall, making money right from the front door. I met this one Azteca princess who lived up the street who would keep me company. We would walk to the small park down the street and make out; she was cool. Her name was Rosalinda; we got along just fine. The boss had to recoup some more drugs and had to leave town for the weekend; he did this twice a month. So I was in charge of the fort.

This one time when he went out of town, Friday night, here came my dear Rosalinda to keep me company. We went to my bedroom and started to make out on my bed. We had the house all to ourselves. I was still a virgin, so I wanted to get my way. Maybe our feelings were strong for each other. I knew that mine were out of control; I didn't know about hers. I guess she was feeling the same way. She finally let me pull her sexy pants down then the little panties. *Here we go.* Before I knew it, I busted my nut. "Sorry, babe, I did not mean to leave you like this." She didn't trip—cool. Then we heard the front door, so we both got up and put on our pants, then she left. I took care of business and sold the drugs.

I felt bad about Rosalinda, that I could not make her feel all of me; she did forgive me. Then she did have her little boyfriend. I did not want any trouble, so I stayed away. So I started to talk to Chica once again. Well, at the home front, all our customers were bringing all kinds of stuff, like new clothes, car rims, and some other goodies. One day, after boxing training, I was getting to the house, and I saw this clean '64 Chevy right in front of the house. I just went inside and didn't think about it twice. So I went inside the house.

Then Robert asked me if I saw that Chevy. "Yeah, so what's up?" He told me that was my new car and that he needed to fix the tranny then she was good to go. So I took a closer look at this cool car—two-door, maroon, no dents, with a small engine. He said it was my early birthday present. "Cool, and thank you." Then we had already had some lowrider rims to put on it, with small 520 tires; the rims were Fenton's. My dreams were coming true to life.

After two weeks, Chica let me visit her at her house, which was beautiful. I knew that she was hard to get, but what the heck, I'd try to win her over. I caught the bus over to her house, Alum Rock and White Road, and made it to her house. Then I knocked on the door; her older brother told me to wait.

So here was the moment I had been waiting for; here she came, looking so fine. We gave each other a hug and then walked to the park close to her house. Then we got to the park, sat down, and started to make out; then it was time to take her home. I was on cloud nine; this was too good to be true. Could this be happening to me? I was so blessed to have found this precious Azteca princess who had liked me too.

So I still had to do the program, doing my thing like going to school and dealing after school. The '64 got fixed, so now I was even better. Now my little lowrider was coming along; we put those lowrider rims with the tennie shoe tires. That made the car drop about four inches; I would drive around the area, keeping low-key. Fridays were the best; I could drive to school and show off in a good way.

Chica and I would hang out more and more. One day, we went to Eastridge to chill for a while. Then I said to Chica, "Before I take you home, let me check up on the home front."

She said, "No problem."

Soon as I got to the house, I saw that the front door was wide open—not good. We had been raided by the cops. So I got back in the car and didn't say anything to Chica. I just took her home and got my tender kiss good night. "Talk to you later." What a blessing for me not to be there at the house when it had got raided. I thanked the Lord. So I went back to my grandmother's house and told her what had happened. Robert just had got busted, so I needed I place to live. She said I could live with her once more. What a blessing my grandmother was. Then I went back to the old house to pick up my stuff and move in with her. The party was over for Robert, but so lucky for me, I was still free. I got my punching bag. I did not have that much stuff, just my clothes and boxing gear.

Now that Robert was in jail, he needed some money for a lawyer, so he was going to need to sell the '64 Chevy. I got a little angry, but it was his. I never gave him money for that car anyways. I was still grateful for what he had done for me regardless. Then he took all the heat without taking anybody with him.

Now I was back at my grandmother's house; she lived in the Mayfair Park area that was right off San Antonio and King Road. They had Lee Mathson right around the corner then the center right on the corner. Everything was going smooth for me. I was still doing my lightweight marijuana dealing low-key.

Robert had taught me the tricks on the game, lessons to be learned in this cold world. I would only sell to people whom I knew and trusted. I started stacking my cash and got more business. Then I found this '68 Chevy, two-door, gold with a clean black roof, with no dents. Then once I got some more money, I put on some small 520s tires.

This made the car look like it was super clean. All eyes on me, baby. It looked show don't you know. I was lowriding hard on my block, that's for sure. While Robert ended up getting five years in the penitentiary—you play, you pay the piper. Ms. Chica and I ended up breaking up. She found someone new; this broke my little heart. Then it was not really that bad; we did share some little precious moments together, better than none.

I was still young and could still pull some fine females my way. I just kept on programing myself. Life was still good for me; I had my school and my '68 Chevy and lots of pretty Azteca princesses at my side.

So living at my grandmother's house was cool, right in the heart of the eastside. One night, I was chilling out in the front yard and noticed this one female who was chilling in her front yard too. So I went and introduced myself. "I'm your neighbor. What's your name, and do you have a boyfriend?"

She said, "No, and my name is Carmen."

"Cool."

We started to chitchat for a little while. She was beautiful in my eyes, and she was blessed in the chest—with a pretty face. She must have liked my style; she gave me her phone number so we could talk on the phone.

Then little by little, we became closer and closer. We shared our dreams of living a better life. I was about sixteen, and she was fifteen, so we got along well overall. We would stroll to the park and hold hands and make out. This was too good to be true; right next door, she was an Azteca princess to me. Then she was still a virgin; I was still kind of one myself. We took it slow as we went. I was busy going to school then going to boxing training, but we made up for lost time. Everything was going cool for a while till she started to cheat on me. We went out for about one year, and she let me make love to her sexy body. So I was her first, as she was my precious Azteca princess. She broke my heart, so I had to leave her. I did not want to share her with another man. We stayed friends, but I wanted her back but had to stay strong. I had to find someone new to share my love with; time to shop around my San Jo town.

I was just getting back on track. I was going to work and school, still doing my little dealing. I started to meet other connections; this one had the high-grade stuff. It was that mean green, the sticky stuff that smelled like skunk, whoa. It smelled the whole house up once you lit up a joint. I just had come up on an eighth and put it into my secret hiding place. Then I saw a cop in the corner of my eye. He got me under in the corner of his eye too. I was one step ahead of him, knowing it was time to make my move. I started to get into my car; soon as I hit the corner of Twenty-Second and San Fernando, he turned on his strawberry lights and pulled me over. Then he pulled me out of my car and started to search the glove box, and he found two joints of high-grade marijuana. "What's this look like, some KJ? Is this a crystal joint?

I said, "No, officer, just some of that good sticky green." Well, he didn't think that. I got arrested on the spot, and he took me to juvie hall. My tio Smiley heard what had happened to me and took my car home. Then the cops found out that it was only weed and let me go, so my mother had to get me out once again. She took me back to my grandma's house. Well, after my mother left, I went and got my eighth out of my hiding place. I told my two tios, "Check this out. Let's roll one up."

"What the heck, mijo?"

"Forget that rookie howdy doody cop. Thanks, Smiley, for getting my car home. Here, now smoke with us, booyah. I say don't send any rookies after me. They gonna get clowned."

Now I felt that it was me against them always. They kept trying to catch me riding dirty, this SJPD. "Let's play this game to the end, baby boys." It was time to stay on my toes from now on, lesson to be learned. I started going to school with a new outlook on this life that I did live. Maybe the next time I wouldn't be so lucky; what then? I started to count my blessings for what they were worth. Looking over my shoulder started to get old after a while, feel me? I wanted to make my mother proud of me for once. I would get caught up in the mix of trouble. Just don't strike me out yet, people. I was not out. I was just down for the count, dazed and confused, in this crazy world that I must live in. I was the same as everyone else, just trying to make it.

In school, I studied most of the basics—math, reading, writing, and PE—always trying to get good grades. I got along with most of my teachers; there was this one who had a liking to me. She was my writing teacher, Mrs. Dunn; she was like a mother. She would stay after class and ask how was everything really going. She helped me out whenever I needed it; she was for real. Sometimes, after class, I was asked to stay after class just to give me a twenty. "Don't get to into the trouble on the block." That really made me feel good about myself, that this one teacher had high hopes for me. She taught us about our forefathers of the past and that we could be whatever our hearts desire if we just stay focused, work hard, and keep pushing ourselves to the limit and stay out of the jail system.

While I was still going to San Jose High, I was still dealing marijuana low-key. I needed to recoup some more. I was running low on supply. I talked to one of my friends who also sold some.

"What are you looking for?"

I told him, "Four ounces."

His name was Robin; he was African, a young Black man. He said that he could hook me up after school, so he gave me his home address. So I went to get my money from the house then went to his house. I got inside and talked to his mother, and she gave me, what

I thought, four ounces. Then I left and told him thank you. So I got home and weighted it out; I was short one ounce. So the next day, I told Robin what was going on. He said, "Don't trip. We will take care of you after school." So I went home and got the three ounces to show them. I took my uncle with me. We got to the house. I got my gym bag out the car and went inside.

His mom just gave me an ounce, so I left. On the way back to the house, we stopped at the store to get some goodies, then this undercover car passed us and made a U-turn. Then the cops started to question me then searched the car and found the marijuana.

They arrested me and let my uncle go. He took my car home for safekeeping. The cops had to drop the charges on me; they had no right to search my car in the first place. Then I had $200 on me, which they took. My mom got me out of juvenile hall and took me back to my grandmother's home. What a close one. These cops were always messing with me. I got my money back and went back to get some more marijuana to deal. Forget these cops.

So I was out of school for the summer of 1980. I started off good; I was working at the shingles plant, making cool money from seven thirty to three thirty. Then after work, I would get home and do a little partying, still smoking weed but not selling it. Then in about two months, work got slow, so we got laid off. Still, life was good in the hood. My great uncle would let me work at some jobs with him so I could have just some pocket change, better than being broke. His name was Richardo; we called him Pancho. He would get us beer so we could drink with him and keep him company. He always had love for me and his other nephews. Well, in the middle of summer, my brother wanted to visit me and the rest of the family, like our grandma. So this one Sunday, we started the day like any other Sunday. I washed my lowrider '68 Chevy.

We ate our breakfast and went to the store for our grandma for some stuff, eggs, and *papas* to take home. We started to kick back, listened to some oldies, and started to see what we were gonna do for the rest of this beautiful day. Everyone was making their plans for the day and night. I just broke up with my lady next door, so I told my little brother if he wanted to take a ride to visit this other female I once dated in the past.

"Yeah, sure, I wanna go with you."

So off we went to Alum Rock and White Road. She said, "Sure, wait and let me get ready," so we waited outside. Her name was Martha; she had a sexy body and a lovely face. We went to the park near her house. My brother, Albert, waited in car, listening to music.

Then my brother asked me if he could move my car. I told him, "Sure, go ahead." So he did. This made his day, that's for sure.

Martha said, "Oh, your baby brother looks like you, just smaller. He's cute."

So then I dropped her off and asked her if I could see her later tonight about seven.

"That's cool."

"Alrighty then, give me a kiss till then."

She said fine and gave me a long French kiss.

We got back to my grandma's house, chilled, and started to drink just a little to kill time until I went for Martha. Everyone on the block was like family; we helped one another out when we could. My tio Pancho lived across the street with his mother whom he took care of—my great-grandmother who was very old, about ninety-two years old. We would show our love and talk to her in our broken Spanish. So my brother was over there visiting, while I was getting ready to see Martha, my hot date for the evening. Then the time came to shoot over to her house. Martha was looking so fine, with a tube top and tight pants and with her makeup. I got to her, gave her a big long kiss, and let her in the car. We got back to my part of the eastside, Mayfair Park. I took her for a ride so we could be by ourselves and got to share a special moment. I also got a couple of brews to get our drink on. We started making out for a while. Things were getting hot, and we couldn't control ourselves. I myself was trying to get lucky and get a little feel. She let me get just a little touchy-feely with her, but not too far—cool. I was so glad that she was keeping me close, and she was a northern star, precious to me. So we were done smooching, and it was time to get Martha back home. So we started to drive through the park, and I saw my ex lady at the Mayfair center. Then I asked Martha if she would do me a big favor.

"No problem."

So I parked in front of the center and introduced Martha to my ex lady. "This is Martha, and this is my friend, Carmen." And we got back into my car. As we started to leave, Ms. Carmen threw a beer bottle at my car; she was heated and very angry at me. I went to pick up my brother and asked my grandmother if she needed something from the store.

"Mijo, yes, on the way back, bring me some milk."

So we all got into the car and left. First, I took home Martha, told her thank you for her fine company, got my good night kiss, and said good night. Now on the way back, my brother told me that this man wanted to drink with him at the park and to come alone. I didn't say anything to my brother at the time.

Once upon a time, over thirty years ago, at seventeen, I lived with my grandmother and her four sons on the eastside of San Jose near Lee Mathson Junior High School and behind Our Lady of Guadalupe Church. During that August, Albert Harpo, my little brother who lived in Santa Clara, was visiting me. That day, we went for a drive in my '68 gold Chevrolet with black vinyl top. After supper, we had a few beers and shared a joint. We retired to my bedroom where I slept on the floor while my brother slept in my bed. Sometime during the night, my brother climbed out the window and walked to Mayfair Park. At the park, he met a man who offered him a beer, which he enjoyed. After several beers, the man tried to make sexual advances on my brother. My brother repelled the advances, and unfortunately, this made the man mad. The man was much, much bigger than my little brother and brutally beat him to death. The coroner stated to me that if my brother survived, he would be like a vegetable. To this day, I still get nightmares and think of him every day, especially the way he suffered before he died. I try to remember my brother as a person full of life. Before he died, he sang a song by Smokey Robinson—"The Agony and the Ecstasy"— from the heart, whoa. My little brother made a very bad choice and paid his very life for it.

I was still in a daze about my little brother's death. We were mad, sad, and angry with what had just happened to my brother. My poor parents were just trying to take it all in, keeping their self-composure, and staying strong. For it didn't seem real at the time, but it was way too real. My beloved mother was strong as my beloved father. Remember, my brother was just fourteen when he passed away. My parents left it in our Lord's hands, while my uncles and I drank to kill our pain—in a good way. For I also left it to our Lord and his vengeance. My mother and father had to arrange all funeral services, as hard as it must have been for both my parents. Then they had to pick out the gravestone, which was beautiful. Hey, I'm sure that my brother loves it. My parents got the best for their baby boy. Then at the rosary, whoa, so many people showed up; it felt like my little brother was a little movie star. So when we arrived at the rosary—I was with my lady and her little sister—we signed in and took our seats. All that I could hear was "Oh, that's Harpo's big brother" in the background. First, I went to my brother's closed casket. I felt the pain. "Sleep with the angels, sing for the angels, my beloved brother." Then I went back to my seat next to my mother.

In about five minutes, my mom got up and started to walk toward the closed casket; I followed her for support. She was in the middle, I was at the rear, and my younger sister was in the front of the casket. Then all of a sudden, my mother said, "Let me see my baby."

I held my mother and told her, "Please don't open it up. Just remember him as he is in the photo. Please, Mother."

So now it was time for the burial of my little brother. My four uncles and I plus a family friend were the pallbearers; we showed our last and deep and utmost respect for my brother, Albert. Lots of tears were falling from my aunts and my grandmother plus my mother. After we buried my brother, we all went to my grandmother's house to eat and mourn. Then we thanked everyone for all their love and support. Then my uncles and I went to the park to have a meeting of peace; I got people who knew my brother from Santa Clara at my command. I spoke to them and thanked them for their love and support. "I shall speak on my brother's behalf. This is my payback, not yours. I don't want any heroes starting any trouble. I still got to live here with females in my home. I want you to go in peace and leave us at peace. I speak for the family. Now do we understand one another?"

"Yes, sir."

"We must be on the same page. Stay strong. We will not shed innocent blood."

Everyone agreed and left back home. Now it was time to get ready for the trial, going to court. There was lots of media covering the trial, San Jose newspaper writing about my brother's killer and what took place at the park that night. So I was waiting inside the elevator when the man who was coroner asked me if that was my brother. I told him, "Yes, I am." Then when we got out, he pulled me to the corner and showed me photos of my dead brother. Then here came the killer. We locked eyes, and I told him, "Payback is a mother." Then the cops held me back. My poor little brother.

So now when I was in the courthouse, they kept us apart. There was very much tension from both sides of the families, which was very common in the murder case before us. Our side wanted first-degree murder, life sentence. Their side wanted second-degree murder or involuntary man slaughter, which would only get the killer of my little brother fifteen years to life sentence. The San Jose newspaper was writing about this murder case. They wrote that my little brother had made sexual advances toward this killer—wrong. My mother just did not understand why they would write all these untrue things about her son. I myself said in my head, *My brother is dead. There are two sides to every story.* My brother could not defend his name from the grave. How sad.

Still at the trial, here walked in this man who looked just like a woman. The killer and him had been writing each other love letters—cool. This was the truth, and the truth always came out in the surface. We all knew this; now everyone would know. Well, he finally got second-degree murder, with fifteen to life. I guess that was better than nothing. At least we could move on now; my dear parents, my little sister, and I myself could face this future. It seemed to me like a miscarriage of justice for my little brother, Albert. While we put my brother's death behind us, we were mourning in different ways. I myself was trying to keep busy with school; summer was almost over now. Then I started to box to kill my anger and stay strong.

I can remember that Monday morning very well. First, I got up from my sleeping. I washed up and got ready to take my uncle to work; but before we left, I thought, *Where's my brother, Albert?* I did not give it a second thought. On the way, right at the corner, we saw all kinds of yellow tape around Mayfair Park. I still did not think about it twice. So I dropped off my tio at work then got back home. My friend ran up to my car and told me that my brother was murdered. I could not even believe him at the time; I thought it must be some kind of mistake. Then Adam, my friend, said to me that he thought that it was me who was killed. I could see tears from his eyes, so I knew he was telling the truth. So we were crying together. What could have happened to him, and who did this ugly thing? He was so young—only fourteen. For only one week ago, I gave Adam a ride to Santa Clara to go to court. Then after court, we went to visit my little brother who lived in Santa Clara. We kicked back, ate lunch, and then came back to the eastside of San Jose. I told my brother to take care and be good to our mother. That was why my friend was so surprised to find my brother dead at the park. See, Adam had worked at the park summertime. So when he found my brother, he thought, *What's he doing over here? He should be in Santa Clara.* Yeah, this was way too unreal but so true.

That was why sometimes I wondered if my brother paid his life for my mistakes. The almighty guilt went through my whole body. I, being the oldest, was brokenhearted. I always felt that I had to protect my dead little brother's reputation. I had to get that gangster respect above all odds; my reputation was first and foremost. Hey, I started to build it up little by little—doing my jailhouse time, getting schooled by the old-time gangsters, and showing them my utmost respect. So they gave me valuable information in order for me to be a fearless Aztec warrior. I guess they were the elders who had been to war zones. Gladiators in their days, they got me ready and prepared for prison—the way things took place and to always stay ready to fight. They told me their own war stories, of how they did their time, and life-and-death situations they got caught in. It was a battlefield out there on the prison yard; even in the jail system, things could go all wrong. This was a really good way of passing the time. Really, this information was priceless to me, lessons to be learned. As my time went on, I began to notice that what they told me was true to life. I was getting into my own fights in the jailhouse, not taking any shit from nobody. I could give an ass kicking as well as get one. Roll with the punches, baby boy. Just dust yourself off and give it another Aztec warrior try. Almost what don't kill us will only make us stronger in the long run in this life's journey here on this earth. If you are free or in the jailhouse or prison, just make the best out of your situation, and things will get better. Just get down on your program, and the time starts to flow on by—with love and respect toward ourselves.

We decided to go watch this movie at the drive-in, *Bad Boys*. It was me and my two uncles, plus his lady. We got a twelve-pack of brews and some smoke. The plot of the movie or theme was all about revenge—that almighty payback for the death of one of the warriors' baby brother. Well, in this movie, the killer went to the youth authority and got a seven-year sentence. The boy who got killed in a car accident was fourteen. Then the older brother wanted his due revenge.

So he got busted on purpose to get to the same youth authority so he could kill the warrior who killed his younger brother; it kind of reminded me of my own brother's death. Finally, they met up in the movie and talked to each other. Then the killer said to the brother, "Why did you not take care of your little brother?" Whoa. That made me feel I did not take care of my little brother. Well, in the movie, they finally got into a do-or-die fight and fought like warriors till the death. That was when the killer gave him a break and let him live then walked away. I thought hard about my brother's death and was thinking myself, *How can I get to prison to deal with my brother's killer?* I was in my own little world and could not shake this feeling; revenge for my brother was all that kept me alive sometimes. I had to make my way to the top of this gangster status whatever it cost me; freedom was no good to me. I wanted him to pay and say sorry for what he said about my brother and for killing my brother. This movie really hit the spot. I was an Aztec warrior.

Well, I was starting to get a little reputation as a good fighter. Hey, but that was not putting that money in my pocket. I was still trying to party and bury my true pain, which was my little brother's awful death. So I would chill out with Adam, the young man who found my brother when he was murdered at the park. We became close; he lived right around the corner from me. I would go to his house, and he knew the pain that I was going through. We would not speak on it, but he felt my hurt. When I would visit him, we would lift weights and get our little pump on. That would last for about an hour. Adam had been weight lifting longer, so he was stronger than me. So he would try and get me driven on the weights and uplift my spirits. He pushed me in a good way. "Push that. Give me two more. You can do this." Then after we had finished our workout, we were off to the store for some beer. We would start to get our drink on to beat the heat. I can remember this one night when I had too much and got sick. Whoa, I felt the room spinning and threw up all over myself. I only woke up all cleaned up; my friend Adam had done me a great favor. He never said anything to embarrass me. I loved him for that—a true friend to the end.

We lived on Sanders Avenue, right up the street where Adam's dad lived. His name was Joe, who stayed with his girlfriend and his stepsons. Adam and I had been kicking back for about six months after my brother's death. Well, this one day, out of the blue, we were drinking in the front yard. Then all of a sudden, we saw all kinds of cop cars go to the house of Adam's dad. They told everyone to keep their distance while they got to the bottom of it. The cops started to put yellow tape around the house. That was not good; it was all bad for me and Adam. *What could've happened?* we were just wondering. *What the heck?* We hoped that everything was going to be all right. Then one of the officers talked to Adam and told him that his father had passed away. Joe had been stabbed to death in the bathroom by his stepson. My dear friend, Adam, was in shell shock—just the same as me. When I would see Joe—when he was alive—walking down the street, I'd tell him, "How is it going?"

"All right. How are you doing?"

"All right."

I told myself that when I got older, I would like to look like Mr. Joe. He was so clean-cut and always had his hair short and had clean shoes. He looked cool for being an older man, that's all that I got to say. May he rest with the angels now. I could feel my friend's pain. So that was all bad for my friend's dad. We found out after that Joe got stabbed twelve times right in the bathroom.

This is the story: His stepson and his friend wanted to use the bathroom to shoot drugs. Joe told them, "No, do that somewhere else." That was when the stepson, Frankie, went to the kitchen to get a big knife, went back to the bathroom, and started stabbing Joe to death. Whoa, yes, we lived in a very treacherous block, that's for sure. After that, my friend Adam and I never spoke of his dear father's death. I would be there for Adam if he wanted to speak about it, but he never said anything to me. I did know that Adam was hurting; he kept everything inside. Hey, that was the way we were raised: hide your tears. Nobody wanted to hear your sad story, for we all got a sad story of our own to tell. It seemed to be like a sign of weakness to even cry—sissy la la. We got to be young warriors, brave and fearless above the rest. I think that everyone felt the same way. No crybabies over here.

Well, I went out and picked up a drunk-driving case in my '68 Chevy. I went to court and got thirty days, so off to Elmwood Country Club. I got to do three weeks in Milpitas. So they put me on an outside work crew; that was way cool at the time. First, I'd get up for chow, then I would get ready for work. I'd go to processing, wait for the boss, and get our box lunch, me and about five other inmates. Then off we went in our little van; we went to downtown county buildings to do the cleaning. Hey, that was way too cool. The time went by so fast, plus we got to eat our lunch at the park—just like being free, in a funny kind of way. We worked till about four and got back to the camp at four thirty. So it was just about dinnertime; we'd get back and eat chow, go back to our own barracks, and watch television or go stroll the camp, lift weights, play cards, get on the phone. That was the basic program for me from Monday to Friday.

That was just a good way to keep busy and make the best out of the situation, which I did get into all by my mistake. Sometimes we would clean St. James Park. That was not too bad; we got to see some real females who made it worthwhile. After about two weeks, I started to know the old program. This one time that we were with the crew leader, he was cool with me. We were right near my grandmother's house, right on the eastside of San Jose, so I asked my boss if it would be all right to see my grandma and tell her that I would be out in a week. I did convince him to do this favor for me, no problem; he was Latino. He pulled up right in front of my grandma's house. Yes, I went to my grandma, surprised her, and told her not to worry. Then I went to the bedroom and found my stash of three joints of marijuana. I put it into my sock then gave my grandma a hug and kiss and got back into the county van. I told the boss, "Thanks for doing me this lovely favor."

"No problem. Let's get to work."

We went and did our work thing till four; now it was time to get back to camp. Hey, I was just a little nervous about going through processing. Sometimes they would strip-search, but very rarely; you never really knew. Just take your chances with the dice, you know. Well, I did make it through, no problem. I told my close homeboy, "We be getting high tonight, baby boy." First, we went to eat dinner and got back to our barracks and made our move. Now that we were high, watching TV time didn't seem so bad now. We were chilling like some villains, just checking out the program. We put away the rest of the joints. Hey, it was Friday night, so most everyone was in an upbeat mood, calling their ladies, drinking coffee, and writing love letters. Then all of a sudden, I heard my name for release. *Was that my name?*

"Roll up your gear and report to processing for your release."

So yes, I shall be free once again, so everyone was happy for me. Then I gave my homeboy the two joints that were left. I got my gear and reported to processing for my release. Oh, what a feeling—that I must say. Hey, who likes to do time? Not me.

So there I went to the bus stop, got myself back to my city (San Jose), and got some beer to celebrate. So now I was out, and I got back into the swing of things once again. I started to make up for lost time and got my smoke on, plus my drink on. Hey, that was all fine and dandy for just a while. Then I would start to visit some females and get my freak on—nothing steady, just another booty call. I do mean that if you just liked each other, it was on. We'd start to make out, then one thing would lead to another; we'd be making love. There were no questions asked, like "Call me," "See you when I see you," and that was it. Well, I was still smoking crystal joints at $20 for one. It seemed to make all my pain disappear while I was out of my mind. I would wake up after, and my brain would still be sizzling, all off-balance. This comedown was nothing nice, but there I was getting high one more time—sometimes ending up in the county jail, still high, and wondering just what the heck took place. It was always for doing something stupid, and I could only blame myself, nobody else. I just kept kicking myself in the ass, making the very same mistake over and over. There were some people on my block who sold KJ joints, which were real easy to get if you had the money.

This one morning, everybody had left my grandma's house. So I was home alone, thinking of all this trouble—no job, no car, no honey. Then I began to really miss my little brother and felt my world start to close in on me. It seemed to me that I had nothing to look forward to in my life. I completely lost all heart. Talking about hitting that rock bottom, everything looked like darkness. I was blind with my pain; I called my dead brother's name. Then I made up my mind. *Today is a good day to die.* My depression had taken over me in the worst way. I felt so convicted and condemned over the death of my little brother. So I got into the bathroom and pulled out a razor blade. Then I looked into that mirror with tears in my eyes and started to cut my throat. Whoa, I started to see the blood rush out. *I will see my brother now.* Then I went to lie down to let the blood drain; I did not care what everybody thought. I felt that it was my life, my pain, and my little brother. Well, my little sister found me in a pool of my own blood, then she cried and called an ambulance. We went to the hospital, and I got stitched up. They put about ten stitches in my throat and sent me home. So that did not work; now I must be stronger. I must live this life out now and make the best out of my situation at hand. I felt that I would've died when I slit my throat, but that was not to be true. All that I could say was that devil made me do it, which sounded weak. That was my story; it was not the Lord's will that I be dead.

Well, I kept on drinking and smoking that elephant tranquilizer, being a fool. I got myself busted, doing my sixty days and nights. I started getting more familiar with this jail life. I guess I was so hardheaded and still wanted to break the law. After I tried to kill myself, everybody on the block never told me anything. That was cool; I did feel bad already over what I had done. We cannot turn back those hands of time; that is the truth. My friend Adam and I would still kick back together and party. Adam said to me, "We got to live this life out, brother, and not stress out this life." Those were words of wisdom for my ears only. First, we would get a twelve-pack of brew and take it from there. Then we'd try and find some smoke and get mellow, just what the doctor ordered. That sure took that depression away for a little while. That was the way the program went. I'd get back home and find something to grub on. Then sometimes I was still smoking that PCP and still trying to stay away from that stuff. That only led me to want to steal car systems. Well, this one night, when it was getting late, there I went checking out the neighborhood. So I was walking, and right around the corner, I saw this one car. I passed through one time then one more time. Then I looked around; all was quiet. Then I made my move and broke the window—oh shit, I started to run up the block. I got myself back to home base and waited for about one hour. I started to look outside. Everything looked quiet, so I started to make my second move, going back to that car. But little did I know, these guys were just waiting for me with bats. I walked right into the trap; as soon as I was close, they jumped me. Hey, these cats were like big football players; they pulled me out and started to beat me up and down.

CHAPTER 3

GOING TO SAN JOSE JAILHOUSE

Right there on the spot, they beat me up then asked me who else was helping me. I told them that I was all alone. They did finally stop and held me till the cops arrested me. Plus there were some of the neighbors who got up after all hell broke loose. So there I was again right back in that jailhouse. I got booked and fingerprinted. They kept me in the old jail; my section was the snake pits. So I was busted red-handed; I'd just get to court and pray that the judge would be in a good mood. I hoped that the judge got some loving the night before—as if that really ever mattered.

When I did first get to go to the restroom, I saw some blood in my urine (pee). At first, I got a little scared, but it went away, thank our Lord. So I got with the program once again, waiting for court. My one charge was auto burglary. Well, one thing that I knew was that I would be here for a while. First was my charge, with no priors, then remand to custody till next court date. It took about three court dates till I got sentenced to sixty days with two years' probation. So I took that deal with a little smile. That meant that all I would really do was forty days total with good time. After that, they sent you to Milpitas to do the rest of your time—cool. There I was once again, getting clowned by my dear homeboys. "Hey, what happened? Went and got busted with your hand in the cookie jar?" I did not care what they said anyways. The way that I saw it was another lesson to be learned. Now the only thing to do was to make the best of my situation, *que no?* There I went to that weight pile then started to make projects. That was the small heart and bootys and picture frames—that was the hustle. People would hit me up and ask how much for the frames and say what colors they wanted. We would make a couple of frames with three dimensions, some with only two or single dimension. We'd make our list for the store; that was where I got my zoom zooms and wham whams. When you are in jail, you work with what you got, and that's it, baby boy. So now you feel a little better with what the future may bring your way. It seems when you get caught up in the jail system, there ain't no way out. Really, it's a good thing, get to clean the system. I was blind to see what the system was doing for me.

Well, I finished doing my time. I got released and was back on the streets once again. Then I was cool for the first week. I started to smoke that crystal joint once again; I didn't know why. My foolish ways. This one night, I was drinking till the very next morning. I was drinking at a friend's house; we called it the madhouse. Everybody went there to get their party on. It was about ten in the morning on a Sunday. It was summertime, and living was easy. This one older man was selling crystal joints, and I asked him to spark one up. He said he couldn't do it as it was somebody else's. Cool. Well, the day before, we were drinking together, and he was playing with his buck knife. See, this older man had done time in the joint, at Folsom. Back to that Sunday morning. We were talking on the front porch. His name was Richard; he still would not spark up one. I finally got angry and punched him in his mouth; he fell. Then the front door opened up; it was my friend's mother. "Hey, what's wrong?"

I reached for Richard, pulled him up, and said, "Don't worry. It's all good."

She went back inside the house. That was when I heard the knife open up and felt the blade go into my stomach. "What the heck? You stabbed me. Now go ahead and kill me." Then he sliced my arm. I told everyone to back up and covered my wound. I then walked off the porch and made it about fifty feet. That was when I fell to the ground, seeing pictures of my life pass over me. I guess I was in shell shock. All that I can remember is the cops asking me if I had known who had stabbed me. I refused to tell them anything, then I passed out. All that was going through my mind was Richard was gonna pay for this. I woke up in the hospital with tubes in my arms and nose. Then there were all the stitches all down my stomach. Hey, I was happy to be alive, that's for sure. All I did was count my dear blessings. I got eighteen little staples up my stomach and a big scar to boot. My doctor told me that another five minutes and I would've been pushing up daisies. My mother was there when I woke up, visiting me. It was funny, for I thought she did not care. Well, she showed me that she did love me and wanted me to live. Then my grandmother was there visiting me also, plus some other dear friends.

There was this one female who was my old lover; her name was Becka. She went to visit me in the hospital, and she was a wild one. She brought me a crystal joint to get high, so we went to the little bathroom near my bed. Nobody knew what we had done, so that was all good for me. I really was out of control, come to think of it. Then I had my other homeboys come to visit me, which was not so bad. They were trying to cheer me up, so they brought me some hard liquor. I got just a little buzzed, and that was about it. I had to stay in the hospital for maybe one full month. I felt like I was locked up for a minute, but I was free. Then I finally got released and went back to my grandma's house. I was cool once again, then I started to fall back into my bad habits, like smoking crystal joints and drinking too much. All the while, I knew that I had been blessed and really did not care. Sounds dumb and very stupid—that I was.

Well, I started looking for work and found some. Good old Taco Bell gave me a chance. Hey, that made me feel just a little bit better about my life. This Taco Bell was walking distance from the house; it took me thirty minutes to get there. It was right on McKee and Jackson, a nice little spot to work. I was still getting high, but I would show up for work regardless. They had me doing the frying, like taco shells, tostadas, and the beans. I think they liked the way that I was working. Hey, it was hot by the fryer, then it was summertime. I even started to try and save some money; I had about $500 hidden in my grandma's room. I was doing the best that I could do at the time. The time at work went by pretty fast, like when you are busy. This one night, I told my uncle to go get me a crystal joint. "Here's the cash." We got high when he got back. The next day, went to check on my money. I had been ripped off for about $500. I had got so angry, I stopped going to work. It seemed to kill all my drive to do good. *What the heck? I might as well do bad.* I got busted more and put in jail.

Hey, lots of the time when I was not in jail, I would kick it downtown. That was where all the action was at. There was this one place where we would hang out at, that pool hall. While we would be drinking and playing pool, I would try my luck with the ladies, flirt and whatnot. This one time, I was getting my game on, and I saw a fine-looking female. "Hey, what's up? You look like a movie star. You so fine." So here I was trying to be a smooth talker. Then "What's your name, and do you have a boyfriend?" That was my way of getting to know them. Sometimes that was all it took. "My name is Chino. Can I get to know you? How about a walk around the block?" Well, there we went for our little stroll downtown, looking romantic. We could see all the night lights and walk to the waterfalls. We'd kick back and talk, then I'd sing to them some oldies songs. "Oh, you sing good." And they liked my smooth style. Then we would start to make out, couple of lovely kisses and nice firm hugs.

Hey, this one night, I was getting at this one young female. We took the old romantic walk and started to make out. Then we went back to the pool hall. I started to play pool, and out the corner of my eye, I saw this other superfine female. I started to ask her, "What's up? I never seen you before. My name is William, but they call me Chino. What's your name?"

"Kim."

So she wanted to take that romantic walk, so off we went. I was trying to serenade her with my cool singing. She must've liked it; next minute, we were making out. Now back to the pool hall. I got back on the table, then I saw both females talking—I think about me. They both called me over to them, so there I went. I thought that I was going to get a big, fat slap. Ms. Kim asked me, "Chino, who would you like to be with?" Well, I was shocked and started to think for about five minutes. It was a hard choice, but I did pick Ms. Kim. She gave me a big sexy smile. Well, now it was getting late; Kim wanted me to escort her home. Me being the man that I was, I said, "No problem." She lived on the eastside, near the Alexian Brothers Hospital. Cool. I couldn't wait to get her home; she had a sexy bedroom body. We got our little freak on. Oh my god, she had some good loving, that's for sure.

Then I ended up getting busted once again. Oh man. While I was doing my time, I avoided any trouble. Then it was that magic time for my release from that county jail. I was getting dressed into my old street clothes. I met this one lowrider dude, and we started to talk. This guy went by the name Oscar. He was about the same age as me; I was twenty-one at this time. We started to talk about getting high and trying to make some fast cash. We both got out at the same time, and we were downtown. We got on the bus, and we were going toward the westside. Then we got off at Race and San Carlos, near the old parole office. So we were walking and talking. "What are we going to steal, brother?" As we were thinking, Oscar saw this one furniture store with nice chairs in the front. Then all of a sudden, he grabbed one. This guy blew my mind. *What the heck?* So we were thinking now where we could sell it for some KJ. I told him that I knew somebody who lived close by who would trade us. Then we made it to the horseshoe park on Spencer. We did make a clean getaway, and everything was quiet. So here I was knocking on my homeboy's door; his sister let me get at her. I asked for her mother and asked her for this favor. She looked at the chair and gave us a joint, and we left the chair for collateral. I asked his sister, Debbie, if she would help me and put flowers on my brother's grave. "Yes," she said and gave me a hug. She was a fine-looking lady—like a Playboy Bunny, very sexy. Then we took off, back to the eastside of town. Then we smoked that joint.

Well, Oscar and I had wanted more KJ; we had come down from our high. So off to the bus stop we waited to go back to the horseshoe. I did not have a shirt, so they would not let me back on the bus. I told Oscar to just go see if he could get another joint. Then I would wait till he got back, so I kicked back at another friend's house, drinking. Then he got back about ten at night, so we got back at his lady's house. He had a boom box, plus some more KJ joints. Then we got to smoke one and got high as a kite. I did not ask him what had happened in the horseshoe. I wasn't tripping on that at the time. Then we split up. I went to visit Ms. Kim who lived nearby. I knocked on the door, and nobody was home. I was high and thought that she had another guy there. I was mad and started to break into the window. I started to look around and found half a joint in the dresser and smoked it. I got more out of my mind and wanted to start to see just what I could steal. I found a pillowcase and got some stuff. While I made my way out of her apartment, I started to walk thinking of my getaway plan. Soon as I got to the second block, I saw a cop car and dropped the pillowcase. I got pulled over and questioned; they found that pillowcase. I got arrested on the spot for burglary. So back to jail I went for doing something stupid; what a fool I was. Then I went to the old jail and got hit up from my homeboy's son. "Why did you rip off my mother's house on Spencer?"

"Hey, that wasn't me. Who did that to your mother? First of all, I got busted on the eastside, and your mom lives on the westside." They didn't believe me. "I think that I do know who did do that. His name is Oscar. I just met this guy."

It so happened that my new friend, Oscar, had got busted too. They found him in the jailhouse and questioned him about homeboy's house. He said that I was with him when he broke into the house. I did know that he was lying off his ass. How could I be in two places at the same time? Crazy. It was all bad for me and the family. See, I had known the whole family from growing up with them since grade school; we went way back more than ten years in the jail system. I really did not think that Oscar knew who he was dealing with. Then I had a bald haircut, like a lot of us did; it was hot. The neighbors said that it was the same guys who came earlier that day. That was a case of mistaken identity. So here I was telling the truth, but no, these gangsters thought that I was straight up lying. This new friend, Oscar, just put me on that cross with my homeboys. Hey, I can't tell you that I wasn't just a little scared, for I was, but I couldn't show it. Then it all hit me on just what really happened that night. Dear Oscar went back to the house, found a friend who helped him break into the house for more KJ, and made his getaway back home. Then he thought that there would be no repercussions for what he had pulled. Then to top it off, Oscar was from the other side—southerner.

South was the enemy; we were from up north. So the homeboys thought that I was a ranker or traitor. That was the prison gangs; they split you up when you get housed. So now I must really watch my back, even in the county jail. I still got to do my time regardless. I had some homeboys saying that was messed up, what I had done. No love for me. I told them, "Don't you believe everything that you hear and only half of what you see." Then I asked them, "Hey, were you there?"

"No."

"Then keep out of my business."

Well, lucky for me, I still had a couple of gangster homeboys who did believe me. Then I did not feel so all alone. They had my back just in case someone made a move on me to try and hurt me. They told me not to stress. "Brother, don't worry. We know that you are telling the truth." So here I was once again doing time for being high out of my mind—doing something so stupid. Hey, as bad as it sounded, the one thing that I didn't do was burn the family in the shoe. At least that was on my side. See, what Oscar did not know was that these men were really active gang members. I had known these guys from growing up with these men; I had already done time with most of them in the jail. I did know this: they were connected, living this gangster lifestyle to the fullest. So dear Oscar got his beatdown— jailhouse style. I knew that I might get myself a beatdown, so I only trusted very true and few gangster homeboys. They kept me strong in my time of weakness, so I stayed Aztec strong.

I stayed true to my roots, that Aztec code. For you see, the gang- ster code was just about the same. The gangster who thought that I had crossed him and his mother was the man in charge of the yard; he had the keys. Also, he had the bag of drugs on the yard. When you were locked up with drugs, you did carry your power. That would mean whatever you wanted done for you, you could have done for you. You could carry out your orders, like a general. You got foot soldiers at your very command. Then when the job was finished, you could give them drugs. Then everyone would be happy—mission completed. See, when you were locked up, there was no way to get away from your so-called enemy—no place to run and hide yourself. The only way was to ask for protective custody. That was like saying that you got no heart; it was all bad, a disgrace to yourself. You'd say, "If you want me off the yard, take me off the yard." That was if you got the heart. I was never scared and was always prepared for trouble. Hey, that was if it did comes my way, baby. So me already knowing that, I was on the leva. This meant that if some so-called homeboys don't wanna even talk to me, that was just fine by me. This only made me stronger, train harder, and do more push-ups. I would punch the heavy bag with strong combinations and use my feet to let it be known that I could throw down, like a true Aztec warrior. It made me feel a lot better about the situation that I found myself in. Booyah. Crack punch. Kick.

This time, I stayed in the old jail toward the back. The television was on the wall; it seemed that we were all forgotten back there. I was not in general population. Well, on one night, I was telling the nurse on duty that I was having dreams of my dead little brother, like nightmares. So she thought I was crazy or something. That was when they put me in a crazy two-man cell. The way they thought that I was going crazy from smoking KJ joints. So I was coming down from smoking way too much of that stuff. They started to give me all this medication. The cell they put me in was close to the main officer on the floor, so I was protected from myself and other inmates. I could see all the other inmates going to chow; they would pass right by me. They would tease me and say, "William lost his mind." That wouldn't bug me. I let them say whatever they wanted. Then I would see some of my old friends who felt my pain. I knew that it was a blessing to be protected. Then I would see my homeboy who thought that I had crossed him pass me and give me those dirty looks—like "I'm gonna get you for that."

"Hey, what can I do to get right with you?"

He would be mad-dogging me every chance he got, so I had to eat all my pride to the fullest. They called it a fifty-fifty cell, where the loony tunes, crazy men were housed. I finally got a cellmate. Little by little, my brain started to get normal once again. Well, my cellmate had too much KJ in his system; he had swallowed a gram of KJ. Then that gram had broken inside his stomach, so he was off his rocker. I really could not trust this cellmate. He might freak out at any minute. See, this drug sometimes gave you that superpower. So the nurses knew this and took him out of my cell all of a sudden.

Finally, the jail down-classed me and let me go with other inmates. This was better for me; I had more company. There were about twenty inmates in the dorm. They all had mental problems, like me. Hey, these men were not that bad once you got to really know them. I was still going to court; I got sentenced to ninety days, so all that I could really do was make the best of the situation. Hey, these new friends whom I was doing time with would take care of me—like get me some goodies from the store and give me some love and respect. So I, in turn, gave them love and respect. That was all that we all wanted—to be treated like men and not like dogs. That was priceless in this world, free or behind bars. We would start to get our little workout on, do some push-ups and walk around the sundeck. I was just counting the days to my release. The time started to fly by little by little; I got all my court dates out the way. Then the tension was not so bad with my enemy. He had other things to do his time, his own problems. So we just got to our own program—he with his, I with mine. I finally got released once again and tried to stay out for some time without getting busted for getting high. Temptation was out to get me.

Was I my best friend or my worst enemy? I was my worst enemy. While I was free once again, I was still up to my good old bad habits, drinking and stealing from the local stores and trying my best not to get myself busted. Maybe it was that rush of stealing and getting away with it for that small minute. I was still smoking that KJ when-ever I can, trying to escape my little world. I was still living at my grandmother's house; I would leave on my own little missions. The main mission was to get any kind of money to drink and get some

KJ for the day or night. My godfather (*nino*) lived close to my grandmother's house, so I would go and visit him and my godmother. They had about four sons who had some lowrider cars, so it was cool for me to see them even if I was drunk or high. His sons liked to party, so I would chill out with them sometimes. My nino knew that I was loaded; he was not a dumb man. I think he knew the pain that I was going through, so he never closed the door to me. I loved him for that. His name was John; he was a military man, so you'd know that he had a clean home. He always had a full fridge of good food and always asked me to eat something when I went over. He always had his grass mowed and had a clean Monte Carlo (car). His sons were in a lowrider car club called the New Style. Whoa. They had won all kinds of awards for their custom paint jobs—plus all the fine mamas. John was his oldest; he had a clean Lincoln Continental, pearl black. Whoa, boy.

Well, this one day, I was visiting John, my godbrother. We were drinking some beers. He asked me if I wanted to take a drive with him. "Hell yeah." So off we went to the tire shop on Alum Rock. We got there, and we went inside.

He told me, "This is my compadre." It was his godfather; we met. Then he told me this was his tire shop.

"Cool."

We were lowriding hard, getting all the looks when we got there. So he and his compadre were talking business; I was just waiting in the lobby. Then all of a sudden, here came this small box with a lot of big bills. I just tried to not stare at all this money. I saw the safe, but they didn't put the cash in the safe. It was about closing time. John and I hit the front door; so did everybody else. So John and I went back to his house and drank some more beers. Hey, all I was thinking of was all that money that just might be easy pickings for me. I just gotta keep my mouth shut and wait. When we finished our beers, I walked back to my grandmother's house. I just couldn't stop thinking of that stack of money. My grandmother lived near Alum Rock and Capital. This looked like my ticket out of being broke. John had it all; I had nothing. Yes, John had been living the good life and living large in my books. I was just jealous, and it was my own fault really.

Well, back to the tire shop. I had just made up my mind to do this. First, I would have to wait till midnight and try and make my move. So I was back at my grandmother's house, waiting with my uncle who lived there also. I told him about my day and about the money. "Hey, Tio, you should've seen all that money."

He said, "Do whatever you feel."

Then I found a joint of KJ in my wallet; we smoked it. I was so stuck like Chuck, thinking about my luck. I was telling my tio it looked like twenty thousand bucks or something. I thought that I was gonna do this job and try and come up. Now it was about midnight; he wished me luck and gave me a hug. Then I started to walk down the backstreets. I knew it sounded too good to be true, but I was high, what the heck. I told my tio that I just might get myself busted trying to do this. Well, here I found myself right in front of the tire shop. I did not see one cop on the way over here. I started to check out the surroundings; all looked very quiet. I waited for about five minutes then crashed and broke the front window. Then I went inside where the back room was. Then I looked for the money; it was not there. All I heard was "Hold it right there. You are busted." Those cops got there in less than two minutes—not good for me at all. I got arrested right there on the spot. They took me downtown to the old jail. It was bad enough to get busted; but now I got John, my godbrother, all pissed off at me. I crossed the line; these men were no joke. On top of all this, my beloved godfather was mad at me also. It was all bad; I already knew that I would be getting a one-way ticket to the big house, that pinta, state time. Hey, what was done was done. I made a big mistake. I was gonna do this time regardless, so what was the big deal? I did not get away with anything. They booked me for second-degree burglary.

CHAPTER 4

NOT LEARNING MY LESSON, GOING TO PRISON

Well, here I went again, right back in that county jail. I should've known it was too good to true. Then on top of all this, it was my twenty-second birthday. What a way to spend it, and no celebration for me. I had no one to blame but myself and my foolish ways. When I first picked up this case, I phoned my mother to let her know. "Hey, Mom, I'm in the county again. This time, I think I will be going to prison." I was still in the fish tank; I read her my charge, second-degree burglary. Then I let her know that I had a prior conviction. See, I never asked my mom to ever bail me out; I got myself in this trouble. They caught me red-handed; I had no defense, just being stupid and greedy. Now the year was 1986. I told my mom to pray for me and we shall see what the judge would give me, county time or state time. So here I went through the process; it seemed like the county was my second home. This was the time when the county put me back into general population—cool. They sent me to Milpitas, in lockdown, barracks 21. I still didn't plead guilty, trying to get a good deal. Maybe I could still stay in the county and do this time. While I was doing my time in lockdown, I was working out to build myself up, doing my push-ups and hitting and kicking the punching bag in our small sundeck. All the other inmates asked me, "How did you learn how to box? And use your feet?" I told them that my homeboy taught me the basics in my backyard and that I used to train in a boxing gym, so I knew the way to throw.

This was a good way for me to release all my anger in a good way. All that I would think about was that monster who killed my little brother. Sometimes my hands would be bleeding from hitting the punching bag, but it was all good. I felt like a true Aztec warrior to the fullest. When I would do my thing on the bag, the other inmates would just gather and look at me. They would ask me if a had taken martial arts. I would tell them, "No, just kickboxing."

One day, when we got off the sundeck yard, this one officer asked me, "Where did you train?" I told him that my friend had taught me how to use my feet and I had trained for boxing in high school. He told me that I should try and train when I was free.

I told him, "Thanks for your support."

He said that he trained with Chuck Norris. That made my day, that's for sure. Then I found out that my other enemy was out on the yard, waiting for me. So that kept me on my toes.

This one day, I was going to court, getting on the bus, when I saw my old friend. "Hey, what's up, brother Birdy?" We started to talk. "How's your family?" And then he said the same thing. "Everybody's doing all right."

Then he told me, "Hey, the word is that Shorty wants trouble with you."

I told him the story; he knew that I was telling the truth. I told him, "Thanks for the heads-up, and much love." So this even made me train harder so when I hit the big yard, I'd be ready. Then I got to court and got sentenced to nine months, with two years joint suspension. I jumped on that deal and went to the main yard. I rolled up my gear.

So I was glad to be on the big yard—so much more freedom. Then I also knew that my enemy was in my sights. So my dear friend Birdy was out there too. Birdy put me up on my homeboy when I did get to the yard. We kicked it real tough; like, he was like a true brother to me. Then my mom sent me some money for my books. I started to find out the good homeboys from the bad. I did finally see Shorty, my enemy; we locked eyes. I was mad-dogging him, and he was mad-dogging me. There was no love lost between us. I got back to my few homeboys, and he with all his homeboys. Remember, whoever had the drugs also had the power. Well, he was the man out on the yard. I knew this was the case with him. He was the general, and he had some warriors at his command. I had few but true warriors on my side; that was fine by me. The main thing was that my warriors were all good boxing warriors. We would go to the weight pile and get our pump on for about two hours. Well, one of his primes was kicking it with me, and he did not care for his own prime. The tension was getting so thick, you could cut it with a knife.

So this one day, I saw Shorty sitting down for lunch. I was getting my chow and telling my homeboy, "Watch this." As I passed him, I started to laugh out loud; this got him heated. I ate my lunch then went to hit the yard; Shorty followed me to my barracks. We squared off, and I told him, "Go ahead and make your move, baby boy. I'm ready to get down like James Brown." He checked himself then backed up.

Well, after he backed up, I put my hands down. I tried to tell him that I was not the one who broke into his mother's house. Then I told him to get off my back. "I am glad this is over with. Now can we all just get along?" We made a deal; I would help him with a picture frame. Then I told him sorry about that so-called friend whom I took over to his mother's house. My bad. We shook hands and let the past stay in the past. So now I could do the rest of my time in peace. I was happy that we finally saw eye to eye after about two years. We started to be friends once again.

Then in about a week after that, his cousin (*primo*) had a little trouble with another inmate. Then I got to the bottom of that situation and backed his play. I told Ricky, his primo, to call him to the front of his bunk. Then I asked him if he was talking shit about him and if he was ready to get busy. Well, fist to fist, we would handle this. Then they squared off; I got a guy at both doors for security from the cops. First, the guy hit Ricky and swung on me. I told Ricky to move out of the way; now it was homeboy and me fighting. So I backed up into my boxing stance, ready for some punch; he couldn't even get close. I *rocked him* with a right hook; he fell to the floor, then I hit him once again. It was about midnight, so everyone woke up from that crack. I got my warriors out before the cops got there. Now the yard knew that I did know how to sling these sharks very smoothly. It was no secret that I was good with these boxing skills. I just did what I had to do. No problem. Ciao, baby.

Then the very next morning, I saw this one officer whom I feel disrespected me. So I was an Aztec warrior on the warpath. See, the day before, he and three other officers had surrounded me. I was just kicking back with my friends. So I hit him up, came out of my shirt, and told him, "You should've talked to me man-to-man." I guess I sort of challenged him; I was so heated behind this. That was my bad, so I had to go back to the lockdown unit. So I got rehoused and made the best out of this situation. He had told me only thirty days, then I could come back to the main yard. Well, when I got to my new living quarters, I saw my eastside Aztec warriors, Birdy and Ringo. Then I saw that most of the other inmates were from the horseshoe—that was the westside of town. So the odds were not even at all. See, back in those days, that was how this game was played. If you had more warriors, you were in charge. They were treating us like hardheaded stepchildren; that was not cool by me. Well, this one big warrior from the horseshoe, his name was Woody. I knew one of the trustees; he lived near my grandmother's. He would always kick down the horseshoe boys with extra food trays. So I hit him up and told him, "Hey, what about us eastside warriors?" So he did start to kick some food trays our way. I thanked him for his loyalty.

Well, one day, I was cleaning the dorm, and he left me an extra tray. Then before I knew it, Woody was helping himself to my tray. So I hit him up. Then I asked Woody, "Why you wanna disrespect me like that and eat my tray?" He got off his rack and hit me; we fell to the floor. That was when I was on my back and cracked him good in the mouth.

He said, "You hit me."

We got up off the floor. Then I said, "I hit back, baby boy."

Then we squared off standing up and left it at that. Hey, he never messed with my food again, that's for sure. My other warriors gave me my due respect after that. When the officer had seen my black eye, they laughed. "What happened?" I said that I fell off my bunk; they knew that I was lying. Hey, I ain't no snitch; what happens in the cell stays in the cell. These westsiders think we can't kick up no dust. Get this through your head: us Aztec warriors do kick up some dust.

After that, they took me back to court and really gave me something to think about: state time. First, they offered me three years; I said no. So I was off to court a second time; that was when I saw the little brother of the guy who killed my little brother. We had a little talk. I told him not to worry about me. "Hey, why should you pay for what your brother did to my brother? I will deal with your brother when the time is right." The next time I went to court, I saw his brother in court. This time, they offered me sixteen months in state prison. I took that deal with a big smile. "Thank you, Your Honor." So now I was on my way to the penitentiary; I felt that I was ready for whatever came my way. I was talking to the older men who had served time there.

Well, I was back to lock down till I got my ticket to prison. I talked to Birdy and Ringo and told them that I would be on the next bus. They told me not to worry and to keep my head up. Then I told them how my little brother had been killed. We kind of cried together with no tears. They uplifted my spirits, so we kept one another strong. I had already served nine months in the county. That meant that I would only have to do four more months in prison. That was not so bad when you'd think about it. It was about December when I got my dear bus ticket. Hey, I was still just a little scared from all the prison stories that you heard. Everyone gave me a good gangster hug and wished me the best. I was waiting in a holding cell, all cuffed up. They called my name and put me on that state bus going to Vacaville, the reception center for new state inmates. They cuffed you to another inmate, so on the ride to my new home, I was talking to the man who was next to me. I was still trying to save face and make the best out of this situation. What a long bus ride; it took about two hours. I, being a first termer, felt like a little boy. I had noticed that the state guards gave me more respect, and that was a blessing to me. On the way over to the prison, I passed through my old neighborhood and my grandmother's house from the freeway. That did feel good in a way. I would be back on the streets in about four little months. The ride was not so bad; I could see all the free people.

Well, we finally got to Vacaville and got off the bus. They gave me this number, my new state CDC number; now I was the state property. Then they gave me my state dress code, toothbrush, and new cellmate. These new cells were so small, but what could I do. So I just tried to do the best that you could and get with this new program. The first week went by just fine; I stayed in my cell and only came out for chow time. Then they give me an identification card so I could go to the yard for some fresh air and the weight pile or walk around. It was like a whole new world to me, with so many new faces. Everyone had so many tattoos, then the different gangs were in there—the Blacks, Whites, then the Latinos. I saw some of my old friends whom I had not seen for years. It made me feel better that I knew that I was doing a short time, for some of these men had major time. They called me a short-timer—cool. After about the second week, I went to classification; they asked me in what prison would I like to serve my time. I told them that San Quentin or Soledad. Well, the next week, I was getting on the bus to Soledad. When I got to that prison, it looked much larger than Vacaville. I spent Christmas in Vacaville and New Year's at Soledad, my new home for just a little while. They put me in the central yard for more classification. There was a guy from Mexico in the cell with me. The guard asked me where I was from; I said San Jose. He said, "Then you from up north," which was the way they separated the inmates.

They wanted peace between the north and the south, so they tried to do the best that the they could. I did understand. I finally got clearance to go to the yard in central. Then the man who was in our cell got moved to another block, so I got the cell solo for about two days. Then I made my way out to the yard and walked around the yard for just an hour. I saw some men out of San Jose whom I knew from the streets, some from going to high school. We talked about what we got planned once we'd get out. Then I ran into some of my dead brother's homeboys who got caught up in this system; we gave our love toward my brother. They were from Santa Clara, and this one man who had love for my brother out of Alviso, his name was Big Lou. He pulled me to the side and told me, "The punk who killed your brother is here. Hey, but we can't get to him because he's in protective custody." That made me feel good. I could tell you why. First of all, he was not the gangster that he claimed to be. He was doing his time like a sissy la la bitch. Oh, what a feeling for me and my dead little brother. Well, they brought me a new cellmate; he was from down south. He got in front of my cell and asked me if I played this gang game. I said, "No, just doing my little time." His name was Julian. So we agreed, and that was that. He had been down for about six years, with two to go. He had a TV and a radio—cool. I had nothing to my name, just a toothbrush and soap.

Then when I went to the yard, homeboys got mad and said that he was the enemy. Then I told these so-called homeboys that I didn't play that north and south shit. "The only thing that I do care about is that punk who killed my little brother, got that? This man from down south lets me watch TV and listen to his radio. Hey, on top this, what have sent to my cell nothing. So stay out my business and let me be this time, will you?" Everyone said nothing after that. Some of the older men said to not trip on those weak fools, so I didn't. A week went by, and they moved to the north yard. So I was getting my new program down. I would stay up till about two in the morning and wake up for chow, get my box lunch, go lift weights about three till four, and walk for a little while. Then I'd talk to the homeboys and play some dominoes. Hey, at this time, I had no children or a lady to make me stress about the streets. I would find a lady when I was free once again. I was just counting the days till I was free, just trying to keep my nose clean and do my workout. My mother had sent me some money; that was real nice of her. So I could by some goodies. Sometimes I would do my workout from my cell and listen to some oldies. I told myself when I did get out, I would start to collect the hard-to-find ones that nobody heard. I was really feeling like a true Aztec warrior now, getting my little cuts in my body. I thought that maybe the girls would give me some action. I was getting close to my release date; it was right around the corner. The time was going by so fast, I could not even believe it.

It was time for my release already. Well, they released me a day before my birthday plus gave me a little gate money. So I was off to Salinas to catch the Greyhound back to San Jose. Finally, I was back to my hometown. I got to keep my prison clothes, brown state shoes, and my pants, plus the prison coat. First, I went to check in with my grandmother and to let her know that I was out. Then I visited my friend across the street and let him know that I was out and about. We caught up on old times and drank a few brews. He had invited me to his new apartment. It was so nice to be out here once again, checking out the fine females. My being fresh out the penitentiary was like a rite of passage—like gangster status or something. Well, we had our dinner with him, his daughter, and his lady. Then he had this movie, *Scarface*, that we watched. This movie sure was like a gangster movie, that's for sure. Then to top off the night, we smoked a joint of KJ, so we got high. My friend's name was David; we called him Oso. Then Oso wanted to hear how the joint was; I told him that behind those prison walls, it was a different world. He kind of looked up to me like an older brother, so I led him in a good way. He let me know that if I needed anything, he had my back. Then he told me that I had seemed harder, more hard-core, than before. I was telling Oso about this north-and-south game that was played, a lesson that you'd only learn from being in that penitentiary. "It's so crazy once you get there and see it with your own eyes." I also told him that when I was in Soledad, I felt like a little boy when I first entered the penitentiary; then as I got to find my way around, it was not all that bad. Then I began to feel like an Aztec warrior, doing my little workout.

So now I had to report to my parole officer and give them their bottle. That was to make sure that I was not on any drugs. Well, the first bottle was dirty, and I was honest with my parole officer. So she gave me a break and told me not to trip as the first bottle didn't count. Then she told me that I must find some work. Then I went to the unemployment office looking for some. I was sent to this little breakfast diner near my grandmother's house. The name of the place was A Bite of Wyoming. They gave me the job as a dishwasher, so

I took it. Hey, it was better than nothing; it was like a pay number, but with more money. Well, I went home and told my grandmother about my new job. She was happy for me, as I was happy myself for my new position. One day, while I was getting dishes from the front counter, I saw this one friend. I told him, "Hi, what's going on, brother?" He was with some of his new gangster friends—cool. They were just getting something to eat, and I got back to work. His name was Raymond; we went way back to grade school. He got married to this game, being a full-time gangster. I myself just wanted to live in peace, so that was what I did—I kept a low profile.

So this one day, I was coming back from testing for my parole agent. I was waiting for the bus and got at this one fine female who was waiting near me. We made plans to get together. Well, here came the bus; we both got on—plus her girlfriend. Then I asked them if they would like to drink some wine coolers and some brews. Her name was Delia; she asked me if I just got out of the penitentiary. I said, "Yeah, been out about two months." We got to the eastside of town, near her friend's apartment, and got off the bus. Then we walked to the store for some snacks and wine coolers. I walked with them to the apartment. We made our way inside and started to drink, then they put on some oldies. We were still trying to know each other; we were making small talk. Her friend was waiting for her old man from work. Finally, he got home, and I offered him a brew. His name was Bobby; we shook hands with much love. Then he asked me how long I had been out of the joint. "About two months." So we were getting our drink on, getting to know one another just a bit. The girl and I started to kiss just a little bit, and it was getting late. Then Bobby asked me what I thought about Ms. Delia; I said she was cool.

He then said, "She likes your style, bro." That was a sigh of respect toward me, and he said she wanted to know if I would like to spend the night.

I said, "Sure, that would be cool."

So Delia and I shared some alone time, making out. Hey, I was hungry for some old loving, that's for sure. So we started to get our freak on; whoa, it had been awhile for me. She had me feeling just like an Aztec king. I was thinking, *Oh my lord, life is good. Man oh man.* Then we went at it two more times; she was so pretty. She had sexy lips and hips and a beautiful body. It was all so good to be alive for once.

So Delia and I had shared a moment of passion, the heat of the moment. I thought that she was sexy, and she made me feel like an Aztec king. We had done a little KJ to pass the time—no big deal. We had spent that weekend with each other. Now it was time for me to get ready for work. So on Sunday, I got a ride home. I thanked Delia for sharing some of her precious body with me. She gave me some more hugs and kisses before we left each other. Well, I went back to work and did the best job that I was able to do. One day, after I was done doing all the dirty dishes, the owner called me to the office and told me that I was too slow. Then he gave me my small check and told me that I was fired. I went back to my grandmother's house feeling mad and sad. I told my dear grandmother what had happened; she said not to worry. So I drank some beer and felt a little bit better. Well, I went back to the unemployment office and got another job placement. I went to the job location and filled out the application. It was for a furniture upholstery shop. They did not call me right away, then in about a week, the owner called me and asked if I could come back in. Then I got on the bus and went on over. We had an interview, and he gave me a shot. I was blessed that the owner was a good man and took a chance with me. This was on a Friday, so he told me to be there on Monday morning, ready to get to work. I then told my grandmother the good news. I was there ten minutes early, with my lunch in hand. They had me stripping chairs and other stuff.

Well, the new boss had asked me if I was just released from prison. I said yes. Then he asked me why I did not have a driver's license; I told him that I had no car. So he said, "What if I let you use my El Camino?" So I went to the DMV and got the driver's manual to study for my driver's test. I studied for about one week and passed my first try—yes! This new job had paid me more money than my old job did. He had me do some pickups and some of the deliveries. This made the time pass fast for me—hey, instead of being in one place all during the day. This job started to get slow, so I was laid off. I said, "What am I gonna do now?" Then my grandmother was going to move to an old folks' home. So I had to find a new place to live; this started to get to me. So I had talked to my friend Oso about my trouble. He told me that he was going to talk to his lady and see if I could live with him. She said that would be just fine. I started to get some unemployment checks, so I had money that was coming in. My homeboy told me about this one driver's job and that he could get me in. So I filled out my application and got the job, thank the Lord. Now I was back on track; I was working, had a place to stay, and was free. So now I was off to get some fine female like Delia to give me some good loving. This job was all the way in Milpitas, which was not all that bad. Then the money was better.

Well, my gangster homeboy had hooked me up righteous. Then he was my roommate Oso's lady brother. So we were like one big gangster family—in a good way. I slept on the couch, which was fine by me. Then I wanted to celebrate, so Delia and I rented a motel to get our little freak on. Then my friend whom I lived with was doing his dealing—some grams of KJ. That did not bother me one bit. On top of this, at my new job, my friend Puppet was dealing also. First, they were dealing KJ then moved on to dealing cocaine. They sold twenties and half grams, so there were drugs all around me. I still always made it to work and did my job. Sometimes Puppet would take some coke to work. We would do lines in the bathroom and got that little pick-me-up. It seemed that everyone was doing a little something. We kept everything on that down low and did that snow. Then I got turned to shooting it up my arm; that was an instant rush, whoa. It seemed that you would always want just a little more coke. It was very hard to control yourself on that coke. You could go through a twenty in about two hours. Well, the connection was right in the house. So I kept a credit tab till I got my paycheck. When you did KJ, everybody knew that you were high, but with coke, not so. Just the ones who were up on that shit knew that you were tweaking. Well, it was close to New Year's night, and Oso and I were double-dating. They set me up with this good girl; her name was Lupe. We all went to his mother's house.

Lupe and I had been seeing each other for about one month. On our first date, we had went to the movies with Oso and his lady. So we got to know each other, and she liked my style. Well, back to New Year's night. I finally got Lupe back to the house now that I got my own room. Lupe was a good girl from the north side of town; she went to Heald College. So on this magic night, she gave me some kitty cat, and I shot real fast. She was not happy, so I told her that I wasn't done with her yet. Plus the first nut didn't count. So we waited about twenty minutes, and I gave her some more, and she was in that doggy position, whoa. Now she got nothing to complain about. I put that work in to make her feel special, like she made me feel. Well, we fell asleep and woke up in each other's arms, so I hit it again with a passion. I did have a reputation to uphold as a gangster lover. She still lived at home, so she had to check in with her parents and said she spent the night at a girlfriend's. I did not have a problem with that; that was better for me. She made me feel like an Aztec king once again. I was blessed with some great sex, that's for sure. I was still doing good at work, trying to save some money for a car. I could always get around; Oso would let me use his car if I needed it. He had a cool Monte Carlo. One day, Puppet and I were riding around on the eastside and got pulled over. I was driving, and we were both on parole, but we did work at the same shop. Then this cop asked to search the car; we both were waiting.

Then the cop opened the trunk and saw this stereo, picked it up, and looked at it well. I saw a small bag of coke right under it. I began to pray in silence. He was so go hoe on pulling us over, he did not even notice it. Whoa, thank the Lord. Puppet and I got let go and got to his grandfather's house and did this coke. "Hey, brother, that was a close one, that's for sure. We are still up to no good, living this gangster life." Rock and roll gangster, this oldie was the shit. We tried to get them hard-to-hear oldies for our collection. Well, after New Year's, things got bad for my friend Oso, and he had to move back in with his mom. So I needed to find another place to live, then I called my tio—who was younger—and told him my problem. I said that I was working but I needed a place to stay. Then he told me, "Let me talk to my wife and see what she has to say." Cool. He got back at me one week later and said it would be just fine. Well, that was a great relief off my back. Everything was going fine, and I paid him his rent money. Well, this one Saturday, I got some money and wanted to go to the flea market. My uncle had a son who was about six years old, and he wanted to go with me. So I asked if he could come with me. I said I would make sure that I'd look out for him. I got about one hundred bucks with me for some shopping, some pants, and whatever else that I might need. So off we went on our little stroll; we were walking and walking till we got to the bus stop. We got on the bus and got to the flea market and got something to drink and eat. We started to walk around.

We had got some soda and something to eat. Then we were just looking at some pairs of pants like some Levi's, for me, so I brought them. Then I saw this one clean red jersey, so I got that too. So we were cooling off from the hot sun. I saw this one homeboy from the horseshoe; his name was Buzz. We started to talk. "How you doing?"

"Hey, I'm just doing some shopping with my little cousin (*primo*)."

Buzz was there with his sister, and she told me that she wanted to talk to me later after the flea market. Then he gave me her phone number. I talked to her for just a few minutes and told her that she looked cool. I asked if she had an old man; she said no. Then she asked who was the little warrior. "Oh, he's my little primo. His name is Justin." Then we left our separate ways. So we finished doing our thing, and I had to take him home before it got too late. We finally get home, so I asked my tio Frank if I could use his Camaro.

He said, "Sure. That was nice of you taking my son with you to the flea market. Justin tells me that he had a good time with you."

"Hey, he's my blood too." Then I got into the shower and put on my new Levi's and went to the horseshoe and got to the house. I knocked on the door and asked for Julie.

"Wait, she will be right out."

Then another homeboy walked to the door; he was Julie's ex old man. We had known each other from fighting as we grew up from the streets. I had been the winner in the fights that we had got in. I guess this was too good to be true. So her ex and I were talking, and I didn't let him know why I was there. So his name was Larry. We were talking about old times, then this other female came out of the house. So she started to talk to us, and we drank a brew. I myself did not want any trouble over this female whom I really didn't know. See, Lupe and I had split up after she broke up with me, so I was single and ready to mingle with someone new. Well, we were on the front porch talking, then Larry asked me if I messed around with coke. I said, "Why, sure."

So he said, "Let's go for a ride."

So I said, "What the heck, let's take this ride." We all got into the Camaro. Then we drove to Twenty-Fourth and Keyes down the backstreets. Hey, I had a bad feeling, but it was too late to turn back now. Then I drove down this one ally and let Larry get out the car.

He said, "I will be right back."

The girl and I were waiting for him to get back. Larry finally got back with the coke. Then he wanted to shoot up right there on the spot; I didn't like this one bit. I was waiting in the front seat, then I saw this cop creeping up on us. It was all bad. I told Larry to throw away the needle; he threw the needle on my side of the window. Then the cops were questioning me, the driver, and whose needle it was. I said, "Not mine." I got cuffed and thrown to the back seat of the cop car. I was kicking myself in the ass. Then the cop started to question Larry, and they seemed to know each other, like homeboys. The cops found some weed, and I said that it was mine. That was it. I got arrested, and I violated my parole. I was taken to the county jail, and they let Larry and the girl go. They towed my tio's car, and penitentiary-bound I went.

So now I was just waiting to get back to the penitentiary. They sent me to San Quentin; it was the new receiving for Northern California. How sweet was this? It was close to home base, San Jose. Well, soon after, I got processed and got escorted to my new cell in the west block. I saw my good brother Birdy on the grounds; he gave me my due respect and gangster love. He said, "I'll get at you on the main yard after you get situated." So the next morning, we ate our breakfast together and went to the yard. "Hey, you got caught up on them streets." I told him the story and my messed-up luck. "Where they got you housed at?"

I told him, "I'm in badger section, bro."

"Don't even trip. I'll send you a lit care package till you get on your feet." He said, "Here, we take care of our own people, like northern brothers."

We started kicking it real tough like gangsters or something. We got top-notch respect from all the other inmates. So we got to talking about the streets. "How's your brothers out there?"

"Everybody is doing cool."

"How are your people?"

"Hey, they all doing just fine." Then I told him that I was in Soledad and the punk who killed my little brother was there. He was doing his time like a little bitch—in protective custody. "So back to this yard that we are at. Let's hold it down and do this time like true Aztec warriors."

He said, "Much love and the utmost respect for your little brother. RIP, baby."

"Now we here on the big playground, so we must all stick together, like bros. I ain't losing no more of my bros. How do you gangsters feel about that?"

Well, about one week later, they took me and twenty brothers off the yard; they took us to the whole shoe program. Don't trip; they were only making us more stronger. Now I was with some real hardcore gangsters who were married to this game, active northern gang members. These men were do-or-die; anything went with these enemies, the southerners. They took me under their wing, schooled me in this game, and showed me the utmost love and respect. I learned about this machine when we did our workout: motivation. It was like the military. We all gave one another love and support. Nobody was special; we were all just equal, making one another stronger with each passing day. See, when I first got busted, I called my job and talked to the boss. He told me not to worry and that I still had my job when I was released. That was way too cool; my job was waiting. I ended up getting sixty days for the violation. Well, back to the hole where I was doing my time. In the first cage were the southerners, next cage were us northerners, then the protective ones. Then they had some who were mixed up, with some north and south. That was asking for trouble. That was when I saw this one homeboy from junior high. His name was Jessie; we were friends from way back. We hollered at each other through the cages. "How you doing, brother?" He said he'd been down here sixteen months. "That's messed up."

"Hey, what can you do but just do your time?"

Well, this one day, when we were out at the yard, there were Jessie and this southerner. So there was my homeboy slanging sharks with one of those scraps. Then all you heard was gunshots. Everyone hit the floor. Maybe three or four froze all movements. Whoa, it had happened so fast, then I saw the guards cuff both of them up and take them off the yard. As Jessie passed me, he had blood coming out his forehead. He said to me it was nothing but a flesh wound. Oh, how gangster was that—a true Aztec warrior. Noble days and noble ways. I had honor and the utmost respect for that warrior.

When we started to get our workout on, this was how we did it: demonstration, inspiration, and motivation. It was like the military song—where we were from, how we came, did we come weak or did we come strong. Booyah, let's begin. First, we did three count jumping jacks—one, two, three, one, and count off. Then if you could not keep up, you ran in place. After this, we would do fourteen count burpees and cherry pickers. I would get a little winded after we finished this. We would all push one another in a good solid way. Then I had Birdy right beside me, my true brother, even in the worst of times; it was like the best of times. Well, the brothers in my squad were declaring war on these southerners. We told stories about our little situations. My story was the punk who killed my little fourteen-year-old bro. It seemed like these new gangster homeboys felt my pain; they would listen. Then we would talk about the streets once we got back to the street life. "So when we would see these scraps, we take flight on sight. That means fight, baby boy."

Then they would take us back to our one-man cells. We stayed locked down twenty-three hours a day. All that I would think about was doing some of that coke. Crazy, I know. Maybe it was the way that I had got busted, so close to shooting up that stuff in my arm. Well, they took me to the parole board classification; they said that they had an informant who said that I was recruiting for the northern family or the structure then that my gangster homeboys were active northern gang members. In my defense, I told them that I had known some of these men for many years from the streets and from school and that I didn't ask them questions about their business. All that I did know was that I trusted them with my life when shit hit the fan. Then I told them that I was short to the house anyways. So I asked them to tell me why I would join the gang. Then they sent me back to my cell with a warning that next time that I came back, I would be slammed down once again. Hey, I lived just for the moment at hand. Well, I was about one week to the house, so my time was going by smooth. When I was getting at the homeboys in my squad after we finished our workout, I knew they got major time over their heads. This one guy who was nineteen was doing a twenty-year sentence, heavy time. They still gave me my due respect even if I was short to the house. When I left, they told me, "Much love for your bro. You carry a heavy cross yourself, brother Chino. Now you get out and do bust a couple of nuts for us, if you know what we mean. We got you, bro."

Before I got paroled, we had just a little meeting with my new gangster homeboys. They said, "We know that you can pull in some females with your gangster ways. The first one that you have some of that gangster loving with, when you bust that first nut, we will be there with you in spirit, haha." They smiled.

"I shall do the best that I can. I promise you that."

They pulled me out of my cell in the morning and took me to get processed for release. They had lost my nice clothes that I had got busted in, so I had to find some hand-me-downs. Hey, it was just good to get released. When I was walking through the other men, I was all chained up, coming out the hole. I felt all this massive respect from the other inmates, like gangster status on mine. Finally, I got to the last gate before freedom. Oh, what a feeling. I was thinking of having some real fun. Well, I did not have anyone to pick me up from San Quentin. There I met this homeboy out of San Jose who had his sister coming for him, so he had offered me a ride back to our hometown—cool. While we were waiting, I met this one other homeboy, *Sal,* who also was from San Jose. We started to get our talk on, and he asked me if I just got out the hole. "Yeah, it was nothing nice." We exchanged some phone numbers, and we would meet up back in our city of no pity for the weak. Then homeboy's sister got there, and he and I left. His sister stopped at the store and got a six-pack of Coronas. We were going back to San Jose now. It was about May, so it was nice and hot near summertime.

CHAPTER 5

BACK ON THE SAN JOSE STREETS AGAIN

Yes, I was back on the streets again, and I was fiend like a demon. Well, I got to Sal, and we were looking for drugs. He stayed near Hedding Street. That was so close to that county jail. So we touched bases, and they were having a small lit barbecue. They were drinking some cold brew, listening to some oldies, and enjoying the weather. Sal and I talked about him going to cop some coke. Then I gave him some money and waited for him to come back. So while I was waiting, drinking my brew, I saw these girls riding up, and they pulled in the driveway. One looked pretty, and she had all kinds of love bites on her neck. I asked her, "What's up, and where's your old man?" She said that she didn't have one—cool. So we started to talk for just a minute. Then she said that she had a little girl, who was playing outside. Her name was Casandra; she was pretty and about two years old. The girl whom I was getting at, her name was Monica. So we were having some small talk. I told her that I was an Aztec prince and was looking for an Azteca princess. She started to laugh just a little. While I was waiting for the coke, I could see Monica putting her chest out, looking sexy. Right now, I could smell kitty cat a block away. I thought that Ms. Monica felt the same way. So I was telling her that I just got paroled from the hole and what that was all about—breaking down the way this north-and-south game was played, that I had to be locked in my cell all day long, and that the letter *n* was the fourteen (which was for northern) and the letter *m* was thirteen, which was for southern.

I was putting Monica up on game, the way that was really played. That some of us live and die by this stuff when things got rough. That we must stay strong and keep our heads up above the rest. I could tell that she was playing hard to get. Still, she wanted me to kick back next to her and play with her daughter, and I got no problem with this—better than being around those knuckleheads. I asked Monica to get me another brew, and she did with a smile—cool. Then I asked Monica about her baby's father; she told me that he took off on them. I started to talk to Monica's mom, and she liked me right off the bat. Monica kept shaking her stuff all in front of me, trying to tease me or something. I played it cool and played my hunch; we were getting along pretty good. Then Sal got back, and it was starting to get dark. So we went inside; he called us to the room to do this coke. Finally, I got to do my coke after waiting all this time. They did theirs first, then I got my turn. Remember, we were shooting it up. Then I saw Monica get hers. I was not tripping; she wasn't my old lady. Monica told me that she just was going to be eighteen next month. So everyone had got that rush from this coke. We went back outside, and I asked Monica's mom if she could give me a ride back to my house on the eastside. She said yeah. Then I talked to Monica. "When can I see you again?"

She said, "Come by the next day."

So it was like a date in a way. Then her mom asked me if I was ready. I said yeah, so off we went to my tio Frank's house. "Hey, thanks for the ride."

Well, before I got ready to leave, I asked Ms. Monica for a good night kiss. She agreed and gave me a nice French kiss right on my lips. So I told her, "I will see you tomorrow. It's a deal." So I finally got back to my tio's house. It was late when I got home; I just fell asleep. Then the next morning, I told my tio that I was sorry about his car getting towed. So he forgave me and said that it was cool. I got situated at my tio's house. It was Sunday, so everyone was just relaxing. I got a little money left from my gate money. Then it was about six in the evening, and I asked if I could use the Camaro to visit this girl. He said, "All right, you just be careful with my car."

"No problem."

So there I went to visit Monica across town. Soon as I got there, we had a brew. We started to listen to some oldies and chitchat. I told her that I still had my job as a driver, that I still did not have any kids, and that I wanted two Aztec warriors, one for me and another for my dead little brother. We didn't do any coke that night—just talked and kicked back. It was starting to get late, so I told her that I needed to take my tio's car back to him. She understood and gave me a couple of sweet kisses good night. So I went back home and called it a night. I did not want my tio to think that I was taking his kindness for weakness. So the next morning, I went to work and checked in and talked to my homeboy Puppet.

"Hey, bro, you got out. Good to hear." Then he told me, "You got paroled from the hole. That's a good thing." Then my job gave me some of my vacation check so I wouldn't be broke.

Then Puppet asked me do him a favor and go pick up his little sister. I said, "Yeah, no problem. Where is she?"

"Off the El Camino then drop her off." Then he gave me the keys to his car. So my job gave me a week off with vacation. On my way over there, guess who I saw getting off the bus? Monica. I asked her if she wanted to take a ride with me. She said sure, so off we went to pick up his little sister. After we were done and dropped her off at her house, I got back to the job and waited for Puppet to get off work. He was off work; I threw him the keys. "Hey, bro, we got to take back Monica home."

"No problem."

We stopped at the store for a twelve-pack of brew. So we kicked back at Monica's house, drinking and catching up on good times. He hit me up, "So how was the hole in San Quentin?"

"Not so bad. Those were some real Norteños, my brother. No joke."

Then he had to leave, and I needed a ride home. Then Monica told me if I wanted to spend the night with her. How could I say no to this offer? I told Puppet, "Hey, brother, I think that I'll be staying.

He gave me a big smile. "Stay strong." Then he left and said, "Will you be all right here?"

"Yeah, brother, don't trip. Everything is cool around here."

Then he gave me a gangster hug with much love. Then Monica and I went to her bedroom, and we started to make out on her bed. I was hungry for her, and she felt the same for me. She was blessed in the chest, and I was packing down there. So we got our little freak on all night; we were like two lovers going at it. She told me, "This is out of that respect for you, Chino."

So in the morning, I told her, "You make me feel like an Aztec king."

She said, "You make me feel like a Puerto Rican queen."

I told her, "I was watching you shake your sexy bedroom body all in front of me."

"Oh, you noticed that?"

"Hey, baby girl, I'm not blind."

She said it was out of respect for what I represented—San Jo, our lady, our hometown. I could live with that. With no strings attached, she was a gangster girl, and that was for sure made for me. She was mad horny like I was too. So we were having sex all day long; she was on fire for me, and I for her—like a match made in heaven from up above. We called this that straight gangster love. We were getting hooked on this newfound ecstasy. Then I got back to my tio's house, and he said that I was no longer living there. That was when Monica said that I could move in with her; thank our Lord for her. So I still was going to work, but I didn't report to my parole agent. I knew that I would be doing a violation when I got caught slipping. Well, I was enjoying my freedom as long as I could. We were still messing with that coke and getting sprung. Sometimes I would be at work and find my way home just to get my coke fix; I was getting bad. After work, I just wanted to get home and get that coke rush. So finally, my job knew that I was getting loaded at work and laid me off. So I could still collect my unemployment check—cool. Then Monica said that she was going to have my baby. See, when I had been stabbed, the doctor told me that I might not be able to have children, so I was happy.

Monica and I started getting hooked deeper and deeper in that coke. We moved from her mother's house and into a motel on Second Street. We would be up for three days at a time, having the connection, bringing coke at all hours of the day and night. Booyah. I finally had to see a doctor to get off the bump I got in my arm from missing the main vein, so I fixed my dope in the other arm. We finally got kicked out of the motel and lived with one of Monica's homegirls. She lived on Vine and Oak Street, the westside of town, near the DMV. Now Monica was about six months pregnant, and we were still messing with that coke. Well, these border brothers had broken into this store up the block, so the cops raided the house and got me for not reporting to my parole officer. So back to jail I went till I got my ticket back to San Quentin. What was I gonna do? Just the time they gave me. Monica went to visit me and put money in my books. While I was waiting to go back to the joint, I saw this one young warrior who knew my little brother; his name was Al. So we talked about old times. That was cool; what a small world. Then I went to the store for some smokes and other goodies. I waited ten days then got my bus ticket back to Quentin and gave Al the rest of my goodies that I could not take with me. When I got to the nig house, they tossed my smokes in the trash and sent me to H-Unit, like a small camp behind the wall—cool. What a relief; I did not want to go to a war zone. They put me on the breakfast crew; two guards woke me up early.

So I was able to get extra chow plus phone time—not so bad. One early morning, we were in line waiting to get to work. This female was looking so good to me, I lost control and blew a kiss. She was hot; she had tight pants, a pretty face, and makeup. I guess my hormones might have been acting up. So later that night, I got a visit from the guards; they searched my locker and took me behind the barracks. They gave me a warning, "Don't be throwing kisses." About a week later, the guard was passing out fan mail; they called my name. All it was was a piece of paper that said, "Baby boy Ruiz." Cool. We threw a spread for my new northern Aztec warrior. Then my lady's people sent me a care package, so I was taken care of with smokes and coffee and other goodies. Now I'd be all right till I got out this place. We went out to the weight pile to do our workout. We had this little yard, northern pride, as we ride upon the south. There was this one joker from down south flagging his blue hankie, real tough. One of the big northern homies hit him up. "Put that away, or we will have to take this to the blind and fight like Aztec warriors." So we got our warriors posted up; they walked to the shower. Then we started to get busy, with our warrior getting the best of this southerner, till they stopped. I got to say that he had some heart, that's for sure. It was not just what you'd do; sometimes you'd take one for the team. They took this scrap off the yard and took him to the hole. The way of the northern warrior was the way we stood, that brotherhood, *booyah*. We all slipped, tripped, and fell; but we stood tall through it all. That was first-class demonstration of northern showmanship; they danced one-on-one.

I was getting close to my release date. Then I got a pass to go to R and R. They found my clothes that got lost the time that I did before—cool. I had brand-new Levi's and some Mexican sandals and a red jersey—cool. Now I could parole looking fresh; once again, I played to win. So I got to sport my new clothes around the yard before I went back to the streets. I guess they knew that I would be back for a violation. It was a short time to the house, about one week; it was the middle of May. My day was finally here; they were escorting me in front of all the inmates. You could see my red all down the main yard—fearless northern Aztec warrior about to be free once again. Then they gave me my $200 gate money. How cool was this. I got back to my San Jo town, First and Keyes, then looked for my lady and my Baby boy. It felt so good to be out enjoying my freedom. I caught another bus to Oak and Vine; that was the last place my lady was at. I got there and talked to homegirl about Monica and asked where she was; they said on the southside with a friend. So they let me chill out inside the house; they were doing some coke. I just wanted to do some myself and get a twenty for my bones then another, so I ended up spending the night. The next morning, I woke up almost broke; I still got about $100. I went through about $60 that night, and that was too much. We live and learn from our own mistakes. I got to find Monica fast.

So now I got the bus going to the southside looking for Monica. I did know about where she might be—at Ram's house. That was one of her dad's friends. So I got to Ram's house, he let me in, and I told him that I was on the hunt for Monica.

"Hey, you just missed her. She went back to Oak and Vine Street."

"Cool. Thank you, Ram. Much gangster love."

Monica was looking for me, and I was looking for her. We just missed each other. So I caught the bus back to homegirl's house. When I got off the bus, guess who I saw? My sexy Monica. We hugged and kissed then went back to her friend's house to chill out. We got something to eat then just started to make up for lost time. Monica told me our son was with her mother, that his name was William Jr. just like me, and that he was born on my birthday. Cool.

We were still chilling at Oak and Vine with her friend; I was not doing more coke. Well, it was getting late, so they let us spend the night and gave us the room out of respect. We were both so hot and horny, we got our little freak on all night long. They called me Gangster Ruiz, for I earned that in the joint for standing tall. Then in the morning, I got more good loving from sweet Monica. Whoa, it was good to be me and to get some loving after all this time. These young northern warriors gave me long love and respect and looked up to me, so I gave it back to them. Now Monica and I had to find a place to live till we got back on our feet. I needed to find some work, so I did not want to play with that coke anymore. I was getting tired of getting busted and going back to prison.

I guess I still didn't learn my lesson about reporting to my parole officer. Now I would be in violation once I'd get caught doing anything. Well, I would deal with this once it came along. Monica's mom came with our son so I could see him. He was so cute and little and made me feel like my little brother was still alive. I was a proud father and would let my son know that I loved him so. So that was cool. Monica's mom had temporary custody of our son till we could get back on our feet. Well, after our little visit was over, we decided to go visit my grandma's house. After our visit with grandma, she told me to go visit my great aunt, so we did. She lived in the Willow

Glen area. I talked to my aunt and told her that we needed a place to stay. She told me that Monica and I could stay with her and take care of her; she was already eighty-five years old. Monica said that was cool and she would help take care of her, like giving her a shower and cooking. My aunt's name was Tia Vicky. She was lonely too, so we stayed and took her to the park, cleaned the house, took care of the yard, and went shopping for food. I liked the area nice, lots of old people liked around the area. My tia just did not want me and Monica sleeping together, so we slept apart till she went to sleep. My tia was old-school, and she believed in the old ways. What a blessing for her to help us out, like an angel. My tia had her brother who took her food every night and checked on her. He really did not like me and my lady staying there at first, then we had a talk. I told him that we would take care of her so she wouldn't get lonely; he agreed.

So little by little, we began to build up trust with my tio Primo, and he was happy that his sister was not all alone. Then my other great tio was living there too; he had a car, little red Pacer. It was an ugly little car, but it did the trick. Let me tell you something about my tia Vicky. She had no kids of her own, so she liked us to visit her, plus her other family. She always had fresh tortillas right off the stove, best home cooking in town. When I was about ten, my mom took me to visit her, and she took me to the fair. What a treat for me. I loved her for being so nice to me while a was so young. She had worked at Del Monte cannery for twenty-five years till she retired at sixty-five. She was a very strong woman, that's for sure. We had a blast at the fair; I know that I did. It made her happy that I was happy. Now I knew that the same blood pumped through both of our hearts. We were part of each other, and I was glad that my lady could give her showers to make her feel fresh as a flower, for she was my flower. Her husband passed away in 1976. He was taking a shower and fell and broke his neck. That was a sad time for our family. I do remember her little dog was a mean little sucker; she loved him so, like a son or something. My lady and I went to get some help from the county, like food stamps; all we needed was some food to help around the house. I would do some odds jobs, but nothing that was steady, better than nothing. Monica's mom got us a little car to get around Willow Glen Park—cool.

My tia Vicky looked so nice after Monica gave her a shower and a clean dress and with her hair brushed. It made me feel good to see her so clean. See, her bathroom was small, only a small shower without a bathtub, so it was hard for my tia—being so old—to shower by herself. So we would take her to the park so she could watch the kids play and enjoy the day. We would speak to her in our broken Spanish; she really didn't speak English. That was so cool. It made me speak Spanish more and more. There was this one time when we were at the park with my tia Vicky that I heard "Chino." It was my old friend David (Oso), so we started to talk. "What's up, brother? What are you doing here?" I told him I was just bringing my tia to the park so she could enjoy the fresh air and to get her out of the house. He said that he had to do some hours for the county.

"Hey, that's cool. Better than doing time."

We got to talk for a minute.

"Take care and be good. Stay strong. Let's enjoy this freedom. It is priceless to me."

We stayed at the park for about an hour, and I asked my tia if she was ready to go back home. Then I told Oso thanks for being such a good friend and to tell his people that I send my love and respect.

My tia told me, "Si, mijo, vamanos." ("Let's go.") She was ready. So back to the house we went so we could let her relax around her home and get her something to eat. Everything was going well for a minute. I was out for about two months.

This one day we were drinking some brews, I got my younger cousin (*primo*) there visiting with me and Tia Vicky. Real nice. So we all were chilling, having a good time. That was when I went inside to get another brew. Then I saw Monica just slap my tia right across her face. I got so angry with Monica and gave her a gangster slap of my own. "How do you like to get slapped? Does it feel good, baby?" Then I told my primo to go give our tia some hugs while I dealt with this wild Monica. "What's your problem? My tia gave us a place to stay. We were almost homeless." So then Monica called 911, and the cops were on their way. I already knew that I was going to get taken back to San Quentin, but I felt that I did the right thing. I stayed and waited for the cops to get there; I told my primo to take care of our tia till I got back out.

"No problem." I got my primo saying, "Take off. Don't you wait for the cops to get to the house."

I just told Monica, "Are you happy now?" A northern Aztec warrior wouldn't run or hide from trouble; he'd deal with it. My poor tia did nothing to get slapped the way she was; she was good to us both. So away I went, all handcuffed in the back seat of the cop car. I felt bad for my Tia, for leaving her, but what else could I do but just face the time that the state would give me? So back to the San Jo county jail till I got my bus ticket back to San Quentin. I was happy about this time; I felt that I was defending my poor tia Vicky. I stayed in the county for about ten days before I got my bus ticket back to that northern receiving, San Quentin; they put me in the Carson section. Then in one week, they took me to receiving to move to another prison.

CHAPTER 6

GOING BACK TO PRISON, SAN QUENTIN

So now I was in the holding cell, just waiting. Then I saw an old friend there who was waiting to go also. We started to talk about the good times out on the streets. They had given me one hundred days, so I had not much time myself. We were still talking. His name was Roy; he said they were sending him to Tehachapi. I didn't know where I would be getting sent to myself; I just told him to take care of himself. Then they pulled me out to the bus; I was going to Susanville. I got no idea where that was—somewhere near Reno. It was a long bus ride; we did finally get there. It looked like the middle of nowhere. So we were off the bus and into the receiving yard. Then I remembered that I forgot my mother's photos back at San Quentin, so I told the man in charge to see if he could get them. Then I started to talk to the men around me. We started talking, then one man asked if I was from LA.

"No, brother, I'm from SJ. That's San Jose."

Then all was silent. It was all in the game that was being played on the prison yard. Before we got to Suzy's house, we had stopped in Vacaville and Solano to pick up other inmates. I did lots of thinking on the ride; we were on the 680 and passed by my old home. It felt good to see my grandma's home, and I said to myself, "I will be out in a hot minute." When I got to the yard, I was on level 2, Lassen section. There I met other inmates from up north. Then I started to notice that there were more inmates from down south, like six to one. Talk about outnumbered. Boo. "It's showtime, guys. They're watching our every move. Let's be smooth." So now these southerners backed away from me and chose the side that they were from. I got my bedding and went to my barracks and made my bed. Then I went to the yard, checking out my new surroundings. I kept myself low-key for the most part. Then I started to meet some of the homeboys on the yard, most of them out of San Jo; we had the biggest car. There I saw a sea of blue all around me; I could spot them out before they got within striking distance. I started to do my program, like going to work out, hitting the punching bag, and doing my push-ups. Then I started to weed the weak from the strong ones on my crew. I told the rest of them that we needed to stay strong and to follow my lead. "Who's the yard rep for the northerners? Let me get at him." His name was Ray, out of San Jo. I had known him from the streets; we were cool. "Then whoever hangs with me has to do the program—weight lifting, push-ups, and punching the bag. This way, they know that we can fight if it comes to that. We just aren't sitting. We put work in for the north." Then I asked if anybody got any problem with this; everybody said no—cool. I got the utmost respect from doing time in the hole at San Quentin, so I was schooling all the youngsters how to carry themselves. So now the southerners started to notice that we weren't playing; we were for real. I didn't want to see them take any of my brothers off the yard. Then the northerners who did know me knew that I was no joke; I was loco.

So I was getting my little car going. We were never scared; we were always prepared. Now I got northern warriors with heart and laid the foundation. "Yeah, Chino, we feel stronger with your program." I got this youngster, Richie Boy; Stockton was where he was from. He reminded me of my little brother, Albert, so we became close. I would take him under my wing and train him to box and work out. First, we stretched, got loose, and started jabbing, then one, two three combinations. "Use your hip when you throw your hooks, like this. Watch me, bro." Then we'd go hit the weight pile. "Let's do this like brutas. We must endure. We shall endure. We must be stronger than before and keep our heads up always when you ride with me, baby boy." Then I lost my little brother, so my anger was still with me.

"Chino's crazy like an Aztec warrior, fearless above all odds."

We must be like one family. One day, I was coming back from the weight pile, going to my dorm, then there was this one border brother wearing his blue hankie, thinking he was the shit. So I got my red hankie and put it on my head. "Let's go to war." Then he took his off, and all was cool. I myself didn't want to catch more time for something stupid. I was on fire that day and knew that I would've cracked the shit out of him. Then I get a ducket about my little son for a child custody hearing in San Jose, so I got ready for this long bus ride back, six hours. The day finally came. I got ready; this African and I were in receiving area. They handcuffed us both to each other. Then we went to the small airport and got on this small plane back to San Jose.

To see San Jose from a bird's eye view was pretty cool. It took about one hour, and we were there. I'd never been on a plane before; it was not so bad, way better than being on that bus for six hours. So now I was back at the SJ county jail, waiting to go to child court. I was in the new part of the county jail, just waiting with no movement. I was locked down all this time in my cell. Then a week went by without any word about my son. Check this out, I could not wait to get back to Suzanville—yard time, hot lunches, and workout. I did get more respect from the other inmates, for I was a state inmate. Then they called my name to get ready to get back to Susanville. So now back to the SJ airport and to our baby plane. "Hold on, for here we go." I got back to good old Suzy's house. Then I got back to the yard, checking back with the homies.

"Hey, welcome back, you gangster you."

"How's everybody doing while I was gone for that week?"

"We all doing cool, staying strong all day long."

So I got situated, and Richie Boy and I were strolling the yard. "What's up, lit Richie? You look like something is wrong." He told me that this one scrap was messing with him and disrespecting him. I told him, "You think you can take his wind?" He said yes. That was all that I needed to hear. I told him, "I got your back. Let's go hit the bag, and show me your stuff." We got everything set up. "You tell that scrap in the dorm after lunch, 'One-on-one.'" Richie was only about two weeks to the house, short timing. So it was that magic time, and they squared off in the dorm. We got our northern warriors posted.

"Hey, Chino. Just like you said, it's on. I got Mike at one door then two others at the other doors for our security."

I told Richie, "You got this."

He said, "Yeah, bro. So let's get this over with."

I was like his coach. "First, jab and wait for your shot. Let him come in, then you let him have it. Sting him then cut loose on him.

Just like we planned it out, Richie started getting the better shots and started bombing on this scrap like nobody's business. All the other scraps in the dorm just put their heads down; what could they do? "Showtime. This scrap is all mine."

The next day, that southerner had both his eyes black and blue. He had to put on some shades to cover his black eyes. Boo. Richie told me, "Thank you for giving me some good training in the boxing ring."

I told him, "We don't look for trouble. Just be ready for trouble if it comes along. We stay strong." I knew that Richie was almost going home, and I was right behind him—cool. Then I got a care package from Monica's people; that was beautiful. Now I could do the rest of my time with ease. We had a small spread for Richie.

This one day, I was getting off the weight pile and going to my dorm when this one southerner pulled me to the side and said to me that he told the other southerners not to be mad-dogging me; that was a thing of the utmost respect on my part. I told him thank you for that and went about my business. I sometimes wore my red on the yard to show that I was real about mine. You might think that I was a target, but I felt that I had the heart.

Now these southerners started to group up more than before, so now we must really stay on our toes. The power went both ways. They had more soldiers than we did, and that was all right. "We will endure, we shall endure, we must endure, and we must be stronger than before. Let's get ready for war." The tension was thick on the yard; shit could kick off at any time now. Now I was feeling the stress myself but still doing my workout, and now I was kicking the punching bag too to let them know that we could do some damage. "All eyes on me, baby. If you want some, come and get some. We ain't going out without a fight." As for me and my bunkie, we were up late at night, making this metal sharp just in case they'd make a move. "Ready to stick and move, baby boy. We ain't going out like no busters." I really didn't wanna pick up more time, but if I had to, I would. I just made the best out of this tense situation. I was only two weeks till I got out myself. Then I got a letter from dear Monica saying that she was waiting for me. Oh, what a good girl she had been. I thought twice about going back to her, and she gave me her friend's number to call her—cool. Monica was staying with her mom in Paterson; that was cool. I did contact her, and we did talk. We wrote love letters to each other; after all, she was the mother of my only son. I sent her a photo of myself right after I got off the weight pile, so I was all pumped up, looking like a true northern Aztec warrior. She was happy to see me looking nice and healthy. Then I got short to the house.

So it was the middle of October, and I was just getting off the weight pile. The World Series was on television, then everything started shaking. There was a major earthquake in the Bay Area. Monica loved the photo that I sent to her and said that it made her feel real sexy and could not wait to make love to me when I was free. So she sent me a photo of herself looking sexy with her hair all done up. I had a homeboy make a portrait of her; it came nice right on my photo album. Then the tension from the southerners was slowly going away—cool. My date was the last day of October.

This one morning, before our breakfast, all I saw was these Africans surround this one bunk and start going to town on one of their own men. They beat the shit out this man then took off before they got busted. We checked our own in the system if they got out of control. They had warned him about kicking back with this queen. He did not listen, so he got his beatdown. They put out a green light on this man, who was a crip.

The day finally got here—my day of release. Cool. They gave me my $200 then took me and some other inmates to the Reno bus station. There was this one southerner who had paroled with us; we had no problems. We kept that inside the wall. We were happy to be free once again. So now I was in downtown Reno, walking the strip and going into Woolworths to do a little shopping for some music before the bus got there. I found this one tape with Marvin Gaye and Tammi and sang some cool songs. So here came my bus to Sacramento; I got on it. That was where I got picked up.

Now we were all together, Monica with her mom and my little son. We were driving back to Patterson. It was so good to be out right before Halloween. I had my baby's mom and my son, so I was on top of the world. Then we got home. We had something to eat, a home-cooked meal, but Monica and I were way too horny. Then Monica's people went out somewhere and left us and the house to ourselves. I really don't know what it is when a man gets out of prison—like that fresh meat and who is the first to have sex with him. That was me, so Monica took me to the bathroom and got naked, and I did the same, whoa. We got our little freak on; we both felt good. Maybe 'cause I had not got some for such a long time; I still don't know. She called me big daddy, and I felt like an Aztec warrior. She felt like my Azteca princess. Then to wake up with her right next to me and make love to start the day—way cool. Our son was looking cuter as every day passed. We stayed at the house of Monica's mom for just a few days. Then they gave us a ride back to my tia Vicky's house in San Jo. So now back at home base, I did report to my parole officer, told her that I was looking for steady work, and gave her that drug test—clean. My tia was happy that I was out and we were living with her once again. We all had a clean start and took care of business. We did some grocery shopping around the corner from the house; it was like a mom-and-pop little store. Then I asked the owner if he needed some help and said that I was looking for a job. He said no, and it was all right. Hey, if I'd want to be forgiven, I must also forgive, like when Monica slapped my tia Vicky. So Monica and I were trying to make the best out of this.

Then one day after about one month, we were chilling in the front yard of the house and here came Chuck, in his El Camino, from the store. He stopped and asked if I still wanted a job. I told him yes, and he told me to be at the store at seven in the morning—cool. "It's all good, Chuck. I won't let you down. See you in the morning." I was so happy that he took a chance with me, and it was so close to the house. Oh, what a blessing that was. "Did you hear that, babe? I will be working close to the house." Almost too good to be true, but it was. I told myself that I would do whatever the boss wanted and learn everything that I needed to. I would bag the groceries for the older customers and help them to their cars then check in the orders from the vendors. My days started to go by fast if I stayed busy on the floor—really, like, stocking the shelves, beer, and other stuff. I had this one coworker, Anita, who was so beautiful, like a star, so this made the time not so bad at work. We were just friends who worked together. My dear Monica was so jealous of all the girls who shopped there. Some of the elderly woman at first didn't feel comfortable with me. Then as time went on, they started to. I would treat them real nice so they knew that I was only doing my job. "How are you doing today? Would you like some help with your groceries?" I just took one day at a time. Then my little checks started to come in—cool.

I was just starting to build up some trust with everyone at the store. I just put in my eight hours, take my little walk home, kick back with Monica, and watch television till dinner. We would talk about how my day went. It all went good; I was learning something new each and every day at work. I got my parole officer happy now that I got steady work. Part of my good rehabilitation process were self-esteem and self-worth. It was not so bad having my little job; having some money in my pocket; helping out with the bills around the house, rent, and other things; going to get our lovely, nice dinner for me and my little family (pizza, burgers, and tacos); and getting along with all my neighbors (they knew that I worked for Chuck). "Real nice of Chuck to give you a job." Yeah, I knew this. Now I could cash my checks right on the corner store and rent our movies; I got money to spend. All we had to do was walk through the Willow Glen area, and there was the barbershop. Then there were so many nice little stores—nice and romantic for evening walks—ice cream shop, and other places. It was good to spend money right where we lived. While I was working at the store, I noticed this one customer's car, a Monte Carlo. So I asked her if she would like to sell it; she said not right now but she would keep me in mind. Still, I would check out how clean this Monte was. I just kept waiting and saving my little money. I wanted a car just like that; it would make a good lowrider with just a little work and love.

Then on Friday nights, I would listen to the oldie station on the radio. I would try and record those rare oldies that you could not find. They would play some cool songs that made my night then have some brews. Well, I was getting my 50¢ raises; that started to add up after a while. Then I always got my forty hours during the week. Now I had money for brews and smoke. I felt it was better than doing so much coke; we still did a little bit but cut it off before it got bad. Everything was going good at work; I would check in the milk orders. Then one day, the driver asked me if I wanted some nasty books, sure kickdown. I just kept them at work, but one day, I asked Monica if I could bring them home. She said, "Yeah, daddy, bring them home." Then we would look at them together. I would cut the sexy ones out and put them on my tapes' covers. I was still collecting my rare oldie collection; we would go downtown to this CD store and try and find some more rare soul oldies. This one time, Monica found this one CD with some good oldies, and we bought it. Then we got to the house to listen to it; and whoa, it had this one song, "Mannish Boy," that was so cool. I had never heard it before. Monica and I wanted another son to name after my dead little brother, so she said to me that she was willing and ready to make love and try and get her pregnant. So what could I do but just take her to the room and put in some work? She was feeling so sexy, saying, "I want to have another baby from you, big daddy."

There is no better sex to have than when your lady is telling you, "I want to have your baby." That's what real sex is all about. Then I really wanted two sons from the same mother so they would be true brothers. So we were so happy when she said that she was going to have another baby—and a baby boy. I wanted a son who was named after my little brother so that his name would live—in a good way. Then my mother would have another grandson. Then I was getting this old house back looking clean; I waxed the floors and painted the inside trim. This one day, our friend from the back came over to visit. He had been drinking and was drunk and was being disrespectful. He spilled beer all over the floor, so I told him to show some respect or go home. He went back home then came to the back door with a flashlight behind him, like he was going to hit me with it or something. I came out the back door on fire and started to break him off and got him to the floor and started punching and kicking him in the face till I finally stopped. I told him, "Go home and clean yourself up. Don't you ever show disrespect to me or my family again. Do you understand, brother? I don't play that shit." The next day, he had a towel covering his face. I told him, "No hard feelings. Are we cool?"

"It's all good."

Some of his buddies came and visited him, looking at me all crazy. I told them, "What's up with you, partner? That was for free, baby boy. I am from the eastside of town, where you show some respect or get your ass kicked." So everything was peaceful once again with me and my surroundings.

Then all of a sudden, Monica started up with her shit, started a fight, and asked me who that female at the store was. Then I told her it was all part of my job. We started arguing then got a little physical. I sure didn't want to fight with her. Maybe Monica had low self-esteem; I really couldn't call it. She was crazy in the head and freaky in the bed. So then I started to wonder when she was going to blow a fuse. We also had this next-door neighbor, real pretty baby girl. She would come out in these sexy little shorts. So I would go outside to smoke; Monica would keep a close eye on me to make sure that I wasn't looking her way. So I would look out the corner of my eye. It was hard for me not to sneak a peek once in a while; she looked so lovely. After this, Monica would start a little fight, then we would go to the room and make love. Then everything would be all right just for a bit. I should've already seen it coming; I guess I was just a little stupid to this. I started to notice that if we were broke, that was when Monica would start to want to fight with me. Now Monica was about two months pregnant, and we were both happy overall. I was working steady at the store for about three months, and we were drinking for the Fourth of July. I ended up getting real sick to my stomach. Then the next morning, while I was going number 2, I saw all kinds of blood and got weak. So Monica checked on me and called an ambulance; they took me to the hospital. They kept me there, and Monica went to visit me.

So during this little visit, Monica told me that she told my boss at work I was in the hospital. I was feeling a lot better, and I would be out the next day. Well, we took a little walk, and Monica said to me that we should both go into the bathroom at the same time and get our little freak on, so we did. Man, that was cool, and it was good to have some of my strength back. Then I got out the next day and had two days off before returning to work. So I still wanted to drink, but now I would only drink Coronas. Then this one Saturday, I wanted to get some marijuana and was looking for a dime bag. This neighbor from across the street knew where to get some, so we got a ride from a friend over to the spot. This spot was right next to Happy Hollow Park. There were a lot of southerners there. I got my red SJ cap on. We were in this minitruck; it was me, the driver, the girl from across the street, plus my young brother-in-law, Donnie. I was thinking it wasn't gonna be any trouble—little did I know at the time. So there we were just waiting for her to get this little weed bag. She came out and said that we got to go around the corner; we pulled up to the garage and wait. It was just hot. I heard the ice cream man and told them that I was gonna get a soda. Then as I was waiting, I saw three guys coming toward me; one had a shotgun. So I ran to the truck and told homeboy it was time to go. I put Donnie in the front seat, then I got in. All I heard was *kaboom* right behind us. The driver put the truck in reverse, and we started to get out of there as fast as we could, then I looked up and saw one *vato* with a rifle aiming at us. Whoa.

CHAPTER 7

GETTING OUT OF PRISON, CLOSE CALL GETTING SHOT AT

We heard gunshots in the back of us, then they got a guy on each side of the truck just waiting for us to pass by. Then there were more gunshots to the doors of the truck. "Whoa, what the hell?" We finally made it home without anybody getting hurt. "What a close call, brothers." It felt like we were in a Hollywood gangbanging movie or something. Hey, if I wouldn't have got that soda, we would've got ambushed for sure, thank the Lord. I told Monica what had just happened, and she was giving me hugs for saving her little brother, Donnie. The man whose truck it was was Samoan, so he said, "This means war with these freakin' scraps." He told me to just kick back with my lady and that he would handle this. I thanked my guardian angel for sparing me and the men whom I was with. He said that I saved his life for thinking fast. "Let me and my boys handle this as my gift back to you, Chino, you gangster you." I guess I got that sixth sense to be aware of danger beforehand.

Then the girl who was with us got back to the house and gave me my dime bag. She said, "What the heck happened back there? All I heard was *pow pow bang bang*, and you guys were gone."

Then I told her what had happened back there. "They got mad with my red cap. Forget those wannabe gangsters, blue raggers." I knew that I had a lot to lose if I got busted, and Monica was still pregnant. Once you'd get out of the penitentiary, that state of mind would stay with you. I knew that it stayed with me, that's for sure. This was northern territory.

So now I got a couple of young warriors to keep close watch on my block. This was for security reasons and to make sure that no scraps were in our area. I told them, "The first sight of blue, report back to home base. Keep this far away from my block." Then I began to think that these scraps lived in the lowest parts of my city, then that made me feel better. Then I met this one warrior who did tattoos. So we got together, and he did one on my upper chest. It was some praying hands with my brother's name, like a sign of respect. I knew that I got to keep this gangbanging out of my head and keep everything low-key. Just as long as I kept programming and going to work, I would be fine. We loved our hometown, San Jo, and that was no crime, *que no?*

Well, this one Friday, Monica had wanted to take me to the tattoo shop and put *San Jo* on my stomach in Old English writing, so we walked to the tattoo shop on San Carlos Street. She knew that I had been wanting to get this for a while. So here we went, finally getting this done; it hurt just a little bit. It took about one hour and came out pretty clean. I wanted it tip shaded with two-inch letters. Then it covered up my scar from when I got stabbed in my stomach. So now Monica and I were happy; she said it looked sexy. It was so easy to fall into that temptation of doing evildoings, so I got to keep on the positive side always. At the store, I started to meet more people coming and going. I just got to keep working and do a good job always.

So if I didn't want any more drama, I must find another connection. I met this one guy from across the street. We got along good—for the most part. We got the first ounce for one hundred and twenty bucks then sold a little bit to start off, some twenties. Well, all was going smooth, then we got this one ounce that was way short—maybe about one-quarter short; that was not cool. So I said, "What's really going on? I feel like I'm being played like some punk." I was way heated and let him know; he said that I was smoking too much.

So now we both wanted to get at each other, so we met in the parking lot. We got into our boxing stance; I was ready to do my Aztec dance. We started to tussle for a minute, and he knew that I wasn't scared of him. He had some size over me, but I still didn't back down. Then we got our ladies there, telling us to stop before someone called the cops on us. You must remember that we lived in Willow Glen; nothing but older folks lived there overall. So I was bobbing and slipping punches, then I landed a couple to his head. Then we stopped and played it safe. I told him I just wanted what I paid for, so he agreed and gave me mine. So now there was peace again around our block; that was good for both of us. Now I got to find another connection who would sell me some smoke. I met this one friend who went to the store. We hit it off; his name was Rudy. He got that sticky green stuff—good for me—and he lived close by.

Well, I saw one of my homeboys from the block. He was visiting someone across the street. "Hey, brother, what's up? How you doing?" We shook hands and gave each other a gangster hug. We started to talk, and he asked me if I still did those fancy name tattoos. I said, "Yeah, what do you want?" His name was Little Joe. He told me that he wanted his lady's name on his neckline. I told him to go get his gun for tattoos. So he went across the street and got the gun, plus some Indian ink. So now it was time to get to work on his tattoo. Then we both opened up a Corona and made a toast to all the fallen northern Aztec warriors. The way Little Joe wanted his lady's name was hard; I could only do one letter at a time. So it took a while, maybe about an hour tops. While I was working on Little Joe, our ladies were talking away—cool. Now I was done with the tattoo, and I told him to check it out with his lady. They both liked the way it came out and were happy. They were getting ready to leave. I told Little Joe, "Let me get at you real fast."

He said, "What's up, Chino?"

"Hey, brother, let me use the tattoo gun and put my son's name on my lady."

"Handle your business, Chino."

"Thanks, bro. It will only take a minute."

"Don't trip."

Then I got Monica ready, wrote out my son's name (Albert), then went to work. It only took about maybe fifteen minutes. It was easy, right across her wrist; it came out clean. Then we drank another Corona to seal the deal. Right after Little Joe and his lady left the house, here came Monica with her shit. "Why did you take so long doing his tattoo and did mine fast?"

I told Monica, "Just stop your shit and act right already."

Then she asked if I liked Little Joe's lady or if I wanted to do her. I was starting to look all crazy at Monica. "What the heck are you talking about? I ain't like that. Don't be stupid." She was looking for a fight or something; I just could not call it. After all this, we went to the room and got to freaking. All was good for just a little while. I was in the hallway, then from nowhere, here came an ashtray. I ducked, and it hit my forehead. Then I wiped away the blood and asked Monica, "Are you happy now?" Then we exchanged a couple of curse words, then we ate our lovely dinner. I was just trying to be nice to Monica and stop us from fighting any more. Then we both got ready for bed.

So now we were both lying down. "Time to get to freakin, my Puerto Rican baby doll." We both forgot all about that silly little fight and slept tight. The next morning, I got up and went to work till lunchtime. Then I walked home to eat, and Monica and I were cool. She made me something to eat. So all was back to normal, then I got to get back to work to finish my day. The day at work went fine, and I got back home. Everything at the house was overall good. We started to watch some television, then we ate our dinner. After we had our dinner, we were back to watching the television to end the night. Then all I heard was *knock, knock* on the front door. It was the sheriff's department, and they wanted dear Monica. So I told Monica, "Hey, babe, someone wants you. Go see who it is." Then right at the front door, they grabbed her and told Monica that they had a warrant out for her arrest. So they started to handcuff her.

She was yelling at me, "You bastard!"

I said to Monica, "I love you too, and don't get turned out in there, baby." I felt that was what she got for being such a witch to me. That would give her time to cool off; she just loved to fight sometimes for no good reason. So now I was waiting for a large income tax check. Then the lady with the Monte Carlo called me; she wanted to sell me the car. First, we talked about how much she'd let the car go for. She was asking $1,600, and she would take payments. It all sounded good, but I had to get my money together first. I got that income tax check, and it was about $1,200. So I went to cash it, called for the car, and told her that I got $700 for a down payment. We both agreed, and she could still keep the car till she'd find another one. While the Monte Carlo was parked in her driveway, it got hit in the quarter panel. Now she knocked off $600, so all I owed was $300 more and the Monte Carlo was mine. She called me and told me that I could pick up the Monte Carlo and pay her when I could. I caught the first bus to her house, near First Street and Taylor. I got there, and she gave me all the paperwork and the keys. Oh, what a feeling— finally driving again. This time, I knew that I worked for this and got something to show. I got it home, and it was good Monica was still locked up. I sure did not want to fight with dear Monica.

So now everything was looking my way. I got the Monte and got some extra money. I didn't have dear Monica making trouble for me right now. It felt so good to have some clean-looking wheels. So when Monica would start with her shit, I could just get in my car and leave the spot. The Monte Carlo was a Chevrolet; the year was '82, two-door coupe. When I got the car home, I started to check it out more closely. She needed some body work, but she ran great. The inside was super clean, no rips. I thought that I got a great deal on the Monte Carlo in my books. I only drove the car around the neighborhood; I did not have my driver's license. Well, Monica got out in about two weeks; she was mad that I got the car without her. Then she asked where all the money that I got from my income tax was. Shit thought that I didn't put away a little stash money. I told her that I paid all the house bills rent, food, and the car. Finally, I got dear Monica to just go with my program. "Don't worry, baby." We started to go to more places and went to visit our son in Patterson. She liked the idea of us having some clean wheels. We would go visit our friends who lived driving distance from the house. I did miss dear Monica; she just better be nice. So we made up for lost time when she was locked up; she was all "daddy daddy" for the first two weeks. Then she was "You freakin' bastard, you like that witch? Wanna do her?" This girl was off the hook sometimes. Then Monica loved to get sloppy drunk, then she was on the warpath. So that was when I would keep my distance from her as much as possible. I just told Monica I couldn't be cheating on her and that I would be true to her, so we agreed. So Monica and I were doing the best that we could; we went to one of her doctor's appointments for the baby. Then the doctor pulled me to the side. He asked me if I was fooling around; I said no. Then he told me that I got gonorrhea. It blew my mind. *What the heck?* That damn Monica must've caught something from another man. I was so mad. She was about seven months now, so I must think about only the baby. Monica wasn't coping to shit; that was just fine. Now we gotta take this medicine to get rid of it. Monica knew the truth; she was messing around with someone else. What the heck could I do but just hope that it was over?

I felt if it was me who messed around, Monica would've given me the third degree. "Who was the witch whom you were screwing?" Monica just could not understand that I was true to love—even when love wasn't true to me and even when Monica was in jail. I had her younger brother with me, so I was always being watched. It was all good; I didn't have anything to hide. When he reported back to his sister, Monica, he could be honest and truthful. We were all doing fine; Monica and I weren't fighting. Monica was getting real close to having our second baby, so she was a little grumpy. I got to be sweet to my baby's mother. Hey, that was all good with me. I must forgive and forget the troubles we had. Well, one day after work, I came home, and Monica told me that she just broke her water and was ready to have the baby. "Let's giddyap." I took her in the Monte to Valley Medical Center.

First, I took her inside and checked her in; they gave us a room. Now the nurses were checking how far along she was. She was about six disepells, so we had to wait till she got to eight disepells per minute. Then we waited about an hour, and she was ready to have our baby. Here came the legs then, booyah, the rest of his little body. "That was good, Monica. Way to push our baby out." I picked up my new son and held him till the nurse took him away. They kept Monica and the baby overnight, so I went home and went to work the next day. I told my boss that Monica had the baby, so he let me work half the day. So I got home and went to pick up Monica and our baby from the hospital. Then we had a little barbecue to celebrate. "Monica, you made me proud, and I love you, Mama." Everything was going fine; the baby was doing great. After a month went by, Monica said she found a part-time job at this gas station. It was on the eastside of town, McKee and Capital. She worked the late-night shift. It was not bad; we could use some extra money with our new baby. After a while, Monica would not come straight home after work. I thought that Monica was up to doing that coke back at work or after she got off work with her new found coworkers. I just kept my mouth shut for the most part. She would start coming home later and later, acting like she was single or something.

I just kept my mouth shut and tried not to make any trouble. Now our son Albert was getting bigger and stronger. It was good to get off work and play with my new son. I stopped him from crying, making his bottle and rocking him to sleep. He was about two months now, and I was holding him. Then Monica came through the front door and started fighting with me. I still had my son in my arms; Monica started socking me in the face. Then I put down Albert and started to defend myself. She was asking about some girl at work; I was trying to get her off me then gave her a slap of my own. Now I was getting the best of Monica then hit her with a closed fist all this time.

"You were messing with someone at work."

I just lost my temper and couldn't stop till I finally said, "Have you had enough, Monica, or do you want more?" We finally stopped, and I had hurt Monica and was so sorry. Like the devil made me do it, she called the cops, and I wasn't waiting around this time. I guess I had been holding all this anger toward her. I just lost control; she pushed all the right buttons. Now I knew that I would get busted once again in the near future. I went to live with my tia; I was so tired of fighting with Monica and just moved out. I was keeping a low profile, just going to work and back home. While I went to visit my son, Monica was telling me to come back home or she would call the cops if I didn't. Now it was April 1. I was at work; at lunch, I went to visit Monica and our sons for a little while. I went back to work at the store. Then in about ten minutes, here came Monica, making trouble. She called the cops; they came to arrest me at work. The cop knew me from the store and let me give my keys and give my paycheck for my people. I told Monica, "That's it. You pulled your ace in the hole. We are all over now. Let me do this time. Fool me once, shame on me, but fool me twice, shame on you. You fool me for the third time, then it's all over with." Monica watched as the cops were taking me away. I was kicking myself in the ass once again. Then I started to think, *Hey, first, it's good that I'm off parole, so they can't send me back to San Quentin. Maybe the county will give me one year altogether.* So now I faced my charges; well, they did offer me one year for all my charges—cool. No prison time.

So while I was still going to court to seal or deal and get sentenced to my year, I saw my old friend Homer. In the holding cell, we were talking about the streets and about our cases. I told him, "I made my sweet deal. What about you?" He said he was taking his to jury trial. I said, "Good luck, brother. This county ain't playing around. They giving three strikes like its candy." They offered him twelve years; he did not want that and took that chance. If he lost at jury trial, he would get twenty-five. He rolled the dice and got snake eyes. "You play, you pay. That's the rules of this game, baby boy." I did feel bad for him, but he should've taken the deal. Then out of my year, all I would really have to do was eight months with good time—way cool. Hey, I was willing to do this wino time, then I was close to home base.

This one officer was treating me a little messed up at first. He was looking at my charges; Monica lied and said that I threw my son on the floor when we got into our fight. So I pleaded to child endangerment—not true, but the only way to get my deal. This officer thought that I was some kind of monster or something. Then in about one month, they took our baby from dear Monica; I got paperwork from the county. Then this very same officer told me how sorry he was for treating me bad. I told him, "Don't sweat it. It's all good." Now the officer asked me if I wanted to be a trustee; that meant helping with the trays and cleaning up. I took the job with a smile; that was cool, and I got extra food plus extra phone time—not bad. So I was doing my cool little program and started to see the new inmates coming in. Then here came this youngster, and we started to talk about what he got busted for and who he knew. Hey, what a small world. I had worked with his older brothers. So I took him under my wing. This way, nobody would mess with him; he was a good warrior. Well, I would still try and keep in contact with Monica and my primo who would let me know how my tia Vicky was doing. His name was Tony; he would try and pick up my spirits and run down what was going on. He was telling me that Monica was off the hook, partying and being with other men—no respect.

He said, "She's being loose as a goose, primo. It hurts me to report this to you."

I told him, "Don't trip."

So back in the barracks, locked down, was where we did most of our time till we got sentenced. This youngster—his name was Pete—was like my own little brother in a way. In order to mess with him, you had to get past me. We would do our gangster workout and just chill out and talk about the San Jo streets and what we were going to do when we got out. It was a nice solid friendship out of respect. I would call the house, and Monica would pick up. She would tease me, "How do you like it in the jailhouse?"

"It's not that bad, baby." I would talk to her and tell her to take care of herself. "Just respect your body."

She laughed. "Hey, one of your homeboys is here."

I said, "Let me get at him." He would not get on the phone. So I told Monica, "Just tell homeboy that I'll be waiting for him in here." Now I was heated and mad, and when I did my workout, all that I was thinking about was this backstabbing *vato*. It helped me get through another day, and it felt good to release my stress. See, dear Monica had some old boyfriends, and my stepbrother was one of them. His name was Andrew. So when he rolled up into my tank, we started to talk—"How's everybody doing?" and this and that. I told him, "Remember your old girlfriend, Monica? Well, she is the mother of my two sons. Feel me, brother? I don't want to hear you talking bad about her, understood?"

"Yes."

"Remember that I kicked your ass when we were young, and I'll do it again."

I called the house and talked to Monica and told her that her old love was here with me. She asked who. "Andrew. I ain't even tripping." So then Monica told me that someone broke into the house. There was this guy from across the street—his name was Pete—and she thought he broke in. I told her that I would deal with him when I saw him. So now I got my eyes peeled back, looking for Pete. Then about a week went by. Lookie here, who was coming to my tank? Well, what would you know, it was good old Pete. After he got settled in, I started to go toward him. "Hey, brother, how you doing? Remember me? I'm the northern Aztec warrior from across the street."

"Oh yeah, what's up?"

"I think we need to have a little talk about who broke into my house. They think it was you, Pete. Pete said that it wasn't him. "Hey, that's cool. I just had to let you know, Pete. I'm not happy about this, bro."

Well, the next day, good old Pete rolled up his stuff and found a new home. He must've been just as guilty of sin. I got better things to think about—what I was going to do when I got out of this place. A homeboy just gave me the paper and said, "Check this out." So as I was reading the San Jo local, I read that so-and-so just gave up twenty-one northern gang members; these men were going away for a long time. These were some friends of mine; these were men who represented that northern status. Who was I to pass judgment on these men? As I was going through the tunnels, coming from getting my final sentence, I just happened to see my homeboy Roy who got caught up in that mix. We had seen each other about three years ago at San Quentin. I was off to Susanville; he was on his way to Tehachapi. So we started to talk for just a minute; he was facing twenty-eight years for murder. All I said was "Take care of yourself, brother," and then I went about my business. This brother gave everybody up; this was a big thing in San Jo, like the headquarters for northern structure and other things. This man who told on all was well respected and was no pushover. He had been known for just taking southerners off the prison yard; he was hard-core, that's for sure. I guess that goes to show you how people change in this life. This was June 1992, and this was what was going on in the underground jailhouse prison system; some people were getting tired of doing time.

Back to my lockdown tank, here came this man they called Farmer. They introduced us, and we started to talk. It was funny as we talked I knew his father, Ram. So we hung out together, and he was back from San Quentin and said that there would be a movie coming out—*Blood In, Blood Out*. He said it was all about lowriding, some gangster movie. It sounded cool. After getting sentenced, now I got to go out to the playground—no more lockdown. I got to lift some weights and walk around the camp—better than lockdown, that's for sure. "All right, homeboys. It's my time to get out there. Take care and stay strong, for I'm gone. I will see you out there on the big playground." So I rolled up my gear then got out there. It felt cool to be in a new location, more room to mess around. Then I got to my new barracks—barracks 6, which was close to chow hall and the weight pile.

I started to get a little situated with my new surroundings. "Yeah, baby boy, this is the lick, brothers." I made my bed and put away my stuff in my locker. I walked around the camp and just checked out this camp. Then I heard, "Hey, OG Chino, you wanna get your smoke on?"

"That would be cool, for sure."

So all I got to do was keep point for the officers. Then homeboy went to the light socket with pencil leads and toilet paper. The next minute, we were smoking. After we smoked, I asked what was up on this yard and who was running it.

Then homeboy said, "What are you talking about?"

"Never you mind. Let me send out one of my young warriors to check out the yard." This northern Aztec warrior whom I'd send out would tell me if there were any scraps out there. Like a spy whom nobody tripped on, he was on the down-low. He'd get information, who was doing this and who was doing that. I learned this from the south. They sent in a scout whom nobody tripped on. All along, this scout reported back to his shot caller whatever he found out about the enemy. To me, it was just part of security and being aware of your surroundings. Now I was hitting the weight pile, getting nice and healthy. So if I got to get busy with another inmate, I was ready. I stayed ready and let it be known. I was doing push-ups, weights, chest, arms, and some dips for more cuts on my body. You see, when you do time, time don't do you. So you get your program down— reading, writing to the ladies, eating good, and staying strong. Then one day, I was talking to one of the trustees; his name was Danny. He was telling me about this one fine-ass female who was on the women's side doing her time; her name was Delia M. That was all; we never touched bases. On my way to court one day, I saw this other fine female; her name was Tina M. She was checking me out, and I was checking her out. I finally got her booking number and shoot her a letter; she never wrote me back. Let me tell you, she was the bomb—sexy body and a pretty face. Maybe that was not meant to bed; I couldn't call it. So now I caught wind that this homeboy just got busted—the *vato* who was at my house trying to get close to my Monica. Now I was posted up, just waiting for him to roll on in. So they called me to processing to ask me questions.

"Hey, Ruiz. What's up with you and Lopez?"

I said, "Check this out, officer. Say one of your boys tried to get at the mother of your children. Tell me how you would feel." It was no secret I was out for that respect and loyalty above all odds on mine.

Then they asked me, "How would you like to go back to the main jail?"

I said, "It really doesn't matter to me. The time will pass regardless where I do my time. I say I'm sticking to this gangster code at all times. Go ahead and do whatever you must, for I am a true northern Aztec warrior."

Oh well, I was on the next bus back to the main jail—no problem. I got up to the sixth floor, got housed, and met my new cellie. I took the top bunk and started to talk to my cellie—"How you doing? Just got rolled up from the camp" and other things. Still, everything wasn't so bad; I started to meet some other brothers. I finally got a visit from my mother-in-law. She brought both my sons; that made my time go much better. I told her, "Just keep both my sons together. Don't worry about me trying to get back custody. Just let me see them and be part of their lives." We did see eye to eye on this and made a deal. Well, in about two weeks, they called me out my cell. I wondered what the problem was; it was a social worker. He asked me if I knew Monica. "Yes, she's the mother of my two sons. Why? What's the matter with her?" They informed me that she had took all kinds of pills and she was doing bad. They had to pump her stomach out and she would get better. "That's too bad. Maybe that's what she gets for being such a witch to me then for slapping my tia Vicky. We all must pay when we play." So Monica was not having a good time after all. So I was still doing my time, and it was going by just fine. Then they took me back in front of classification and took me back to the camp. That was way cool, so now I was lifting weights, getting back in the groove. I guess I was out there for about a month.

Then these youngsters hit me up. "Chino, we think this one *vato* is a scrap."

I asked them, "Why you come to me?" I guess they looked up to me in a gangster way; I just didn't know. So I told them, "Let's go handle your business." So we were outside the barracks, then I hit him up. "Where you from? Come out of your shirt." This way, I could see if he had tattoos that said one three.

Homeboy was clean, then all of a sudden, this one youngster cracked him. I tried to control the situation. I asked the youngster, "Why did you do that, bro?" Then I told this *vato*, "Maybe it's better just to get off this yard." Well, in about half an hour, here came two officers, and they booked me for that. "What the heck? What did I do?" I just rolled up my gear and got taken back to the main jail. *Man oh man. Just part of the program. Can't cry about it now.* Now I was down to just three more months, baby boy. I got back to the sixth floor and got housed with a new cellie. "Hey, what's up, brother? Just got rolled up for nothing." So we started to talk and got our little workout on. Then we started to meet some more brothers. I was calling the house and checking in with my tia. "How's everything going out on the streets?" That was cool. We talked and kept it short; calling collect could cost major cash. I got money in my books and got my Monte Carlo waiting for me, so things wasn't looking that bad for me once I got out. Then we were having little spreads and breaking bread, just trying to get off this roller coaster ride, up and down.

Now it was all downhill from here on out. I met this one youngster who wanted to hook me up with a female. His name was Creeper. The girl's name was Lisa; we got to talk on the phone. She said that I could write to her; that was cool. Then she said maybe we'd get together when I got out. It's funny with some females who want to get with a man who is locked up. Then when he gets out, they want to be the first to make love to him—maybe for bragging rights or something. While that was cool with me, I just didn't want to be lonely when I was free. Ms. Lisa sounded like a nice freak female to kick it with. Hey, maybe I might get lucky and get some kitty cat, who knows. So I saw a little photo of her, and she looked good. Yes, sir, she could keep me warm all over, that's for sure. I was spitting game, hoping that she'd like my style. The way that I carried myself was with the utmost respect. Just like fishing, I put out the bait and waited for a bite then reeled her in. I got a live one with Lisa. She knew that I was getting close to the house, so she wasn't going to wait too long. So we were writing to each other. I thought that she was a wild one. That was cool with me; I really couldn't be to choosy then, *que no?*

So as we were programing, some new-arrivals inmates came in. I saw this one inmate who kept on looking at me all sideways. Oh yeah, now I remembered him. Well, a couple of years back, I was doing this wino time. I was doing sixty days, then I got out of jail with some of my jail property. It was in a small lunch box. It had some jailhouse drawings on envelopes. Then I stopped at this bar and got a beer. All of a sudden, I noticed these two border brothers kept on checking me out. So I went to see what the problem was. They told me that I looked like the man who burned them. Well then, I said, "I was in jail and just got out, understand?" Hell no, they kept thinking it was me. They tried to play me out of pocket, then I decided to leave to avoid any trouble. As I was leaving the bar, they both started to follow me outside. I started to run away; for about a block, they chased me. Now I just waited for this one border brother. I let him catch up to me. "So now what's up?" He stole one and hit me on my chin. Well, I got heated after that and started to hit him back—*crack, crack*—then he hit the floor. So I started to kick him in the face, and he was feeling me real tough. I was so mad. "I will rob you now." I took his money out of his pockets. Like a strong-armed robbery, now he could say that I really had robbed him. He had about twenty bucks on him; I took it all for my troubles. "How do you like that?" Then I saw his buddy. I said, "Come here, baby boy. Wanna taste?" He ran off into the dark, and I let this border brother go. Well, the next day, I saw them both downtown; one had a towel over his head. My feet were sore from beating on this boy, all the kicking. Then they saw me. I yelled from across the street, "Want some more? It's for free."

When I saw him in the county jail, he told me, "It's all good."

"Hey, that's just what I thought." So I got back to my program. I was getting so short to the house; Lisa and I were still keeping in touch. I asked her if I could visit her when I did finally get out; she said, "For sure." She told me to come on down, so now I got my foot in the door. It was something to look forward to when I touched down. Even in jail, things aren't so bad; just take one day at a time. Then there's being aware that some of these other inmates are getting long time.

CHAPTER 8

OUT AND ABOUT AFTER
A YEAR OF LOCKUP

Now I was just counting down the weeks then the days away from freedom. Then all I heard was "Roll up your gear, Ruiz. Get ready for your release."

"Yes, baby boys, it's that magic day on mine—December 1, 1992. I'm busting out. All right, brothers, stay strong. Say your prayers with much love from me to you. Shaw, booyah, for I do, San Jo, love you." Yeah, I was back on these lovely San Jo streets again. First, I did kiss the ground. "Thank you, God, for keeping me safe and sound. Now I'm touching down." So now I caught the bus to downtown. Everybody was having a good time, waiting at the next bus stop, going to Eastridge mall. After I got to Eastridge mall, I got off the bus and started walking to my tia's from there.

I got to my tia's house and rang the doorbell. "Hey, it's me. Just got out."

"Come in, mijo, and let's get some real food in your system."

So we ate and had some brews. I went to my room and got situated for the night. Before I went to sleep, we got our smoke on with my tios. Now they told me, "Come out of your shirt, mijo, so we can see if you was putting in work." That meant working out on the weight pile and doing push-ups.

"No problem. Check me out, looking like a northern Aztec warrior." Well, the check was good, all the way around. For at times,

97

your own family members would want to make sure that you were telling the truth. I could've said that I was working out from day 1, but I was really being lazy, just doing my time. I saw it as a sign of respect to our elders, older family members. Say that you are nice and healthy, then you got a better chance of finding work in the future—healthy mind and body, looking strong and feeling good about yourself. Who do you think is the boss going to hire, the weak or the strong? Who will I hire? The stronger man will always win overall.

So we were chilling out, smoking weed. Then they let me listen to these hard-to-find oldies—"I Destroyed Your Love," "Let's Make Up for Lost Time," and so many more cool songs. These songs were to get close to the females, that's for sure. Then if "I Destroyed Your Love for Me" didn't do the trick, forget about it. You might as well throw in the towel and give up on her. So after I touched bases at home base, I got my keys for the Monte and took a drive to see Lisa; I got my oldies with me. I told my tia that I would be gone to visit Lisa. Then my tia told me to be careful out there. I told my tia that I would call her if anything happened.

Before I'd go see Lisa, I would go to the store and see about my old job. "Hey, Chuck, what's up? How are you doing, boss?"

"I'm okay, Chino. How are you doing?"

"I'm looking for work." Chuck told me that he was ready to sell the store. "Hey, that's too bad." Chuck told me that he couldn't make money here. "I guess, I understand," I told him. Then out of nowhere, Chuck gave me a card with some money in it. He said it was from some of the customers; that was right on time. There was about sixty bucks; hey, that was way too cool. That was a true blessing from the older females who grew to love me. What a blessing that I always treated them so nice; it really paid off in the long run, *que no*? So I told him, "Please thank them all for everything. Much love and God bless." Then I saw Chuck's daughter, GiGi, and she gave me a hug and said, "It's good to see you, Chino." GiGi told me to look at the news tonight and to not be surprised if I saw her; she worked backstage. "All right then, I shall keep my eyes peeled, looking for you. Thanks, Chuck, for all your love and support." We gave each other a hug and said goodbye.

So now I got a little money to function for a while. I called Ms. Lisa. "Hey, girl, I'm out and about. Can I come and visit you?" She said to come on down and that she would be waiting for me. So I found her house and parked the Monte. "Hey, Lisa. How you doing, you little star?" She was looking so very pretty. We went to the store for some brews and something to eat. We got back to her house and started to drink and listen to my oldies. It was all good. She had some of her other girlfriends there; so we weren't all alone. Then it was about midnight, and one of her friends wanted a ride to pick up some KJ joints, so they asked me. Hey, what could I do? "Just show me where you need to go. Get in the car. Giddyap." I was with a carload of people, going to the eastside, up to no good. I was praying all the way. Thank God, everything went smooth. They got their stuff, and we came back to Lisa's house. So the girls went to the room to get their smoke on. I was cool with my brews and the oldies. So here came these other warriors whom she knew; I had known one of them to be from the Mayfair Park. "Hey, David. What's up, mijo?"

He said, "Just doing the do. What about you, Chino?"

"I just got out after doing a year in the county." Then I told him that I was trying to get close to Lisa. Yeah, she was an Azteca princess, for sure. We opened up a brew and drank and chitchatted about how was everything. Then he asked about the Monte, and we went outside to check it out. "Yeah, she needs work on the quarter panel and a paint job." After the brew, David was ready to leave, then maybe Lisa and I could be alone. Then I told David bye and to send my love and respect to his family; we gave each other a gangster hug. "Hey, Lisa, come here and get close. I'm getting lonely all by myself." She came to me, and we started to make out, then she took me to her little bedroom. So now things were getting hot, but we took it slow and got just a little grind on with kissing and feeling. Whoa, it had been a long time for me. Then I didn't wanna scare her, so I played the part and showed all my respect. It felt good just to have her in my arms, and the kissing was cool too. Then she said, "Have me, you gangster you." Hey, I hadn't had no sugar for a long time. Well then, I guess she was feeling horny, like I was, and let me have my way. Soon as I got inside of her, maybe five minutes, I busted my first nut. My toes just curled. "Yes, baby girl." Lisa wasn't hating it, that's for sure; it made her toes curl too. After that, we took a little break and kicked back in her room. We fell asleep in each other's arms. It was cool to have some old sugar after doing that eight months.

Then the next morning, we made love—you know, how you'd wake up with that morning woody. I had Lisa next to me; what could I do? Then we got out of bed to wash up, and then she took off with her friends. Well, at least she let me chill out at her house. The phone rang, and I got it. "Hey, who's this?"

It was a female. "Is Lisa there?"

"She took off. She will be back later." Then she asked who I was. "They call me Chino."

She said, "It's me, Renee. Don't you remember me?"

"Hey, now I remember you. I used to work with your stepfather. So how you doing?" So we started to chop it up (talk) for a little while.

"Chino, come and chill with me. I'll give you my address."

I wrote it down and told Renee that I would be there later. Cool. So I got my stuff together and got ready to leave to go give Renee a visit. I finally found her little apartment, and she greeted me with a hug and a sexy smile. First, when I got there, I saw my other friend there too—Dave (Oso). He had given me a place to live a couple of years earlier. So we got at each other and gave each other a gangster hug. I told him that I just got out after doing eight long months. He had a Monte Carlo too; his was super clean.

"What you doing around here?"

"I came to see Renee."

"Cool." Oso told me that his sister-in-law lived with Renee; that was why he was over. Then he took off, and Renee and I went to the store for something to drink, like a twelve-pack of brews. We came back from the store and started to drink out on the front porch, just talking and drinking. When Renee's boyfriend came to check up on her, they fought, then he left. So Renee and I kept on drinking, then it was getting late. So we went inside and drank; she was playing some cool oldies that I hadn't even heard before. Then about midnight, she told Bug good night, and we went to her bedroom.

I was just following her lead, and she got into this sexy teddy bear outfit—how cool was that? She was setting the mood, that's for sure. We started to make out, and now we were lying on the bed. She liked raping me, and I didn't mind at all. "Do your thing, baby girl. Let me rock your world." I started to make love to her sexy body. I opened up her soft, silky legs and got busy. We went at it for just a little while till I busted one. Whoa. Then we opened up another brew, and in a while, we were on it again. I got her in that doggy style, and we ground till I busted my second one. She got me feeling like an Aztec king now; she was feeling all of me now. Well, what would you know, we weren't done yet. She let me bust my third nut, and oh my god, she was feeling like a sexy little Azteca queen. Then we went to sleep in each other's arms. "Oh, what a night to love you dear and to have you near."

Renee said, "Chino, you put it down like a gangster. You got me feeling all fuzzy inside all night long."

"Well, whoa, girl, you got fire in between them legs, that's for sure. Call me the fireman who puts out that hot fire, Renee."

We started to laugh, and she made me some breakfast. Then we all ate.

"Chino, why you keep it gangster all the time?"

"Guess it's in my blood. I can't call it."

"Yeah, yeah, you tell that to all your lovers, boy."

Renee and I chilled out one more night. I told her, "Let me get back on my feet, baby girl." As nice as it was, I needed to get back to home base, my tia's house. She gave me some more sugar before I went, then she gave me her phone number. When I got back to my tia's house, I first hopped in the shower, ate, then worked out. I stayed home for about two days. My tia had her own housecleaning business, so she let me make a little money—cool. I loved her for that; now I could make some moves—like put some gas in the car and have some spending money. Then I started to think about Ms. Renee letting me bust three nuts; she made me feel like a million bucks. I was so blessed, and I thanked God for being so good to me. Then a friend had told me about this part-time job at HoneyBaked Ham in Palo Alto. I went and got this short gig; it paid about $5.50

an hour. I took it with a smile—better than nothing. I was still doing my thing with Renee, and it was going all right.

Dave and his lady came to visit me at my tia's house and invited me to go have dinner over at his house—cool. During my visit with Dave (Oso), he needed a ride to do a drop-off. "Giddyap." So here we went to drop off some weed to one of his customers; everything went smooth. Then he gave me a small sack plus ten bucks for gas. "Cool, brother." Now we could eat some dinner and drink some brews. My part-time job was almost over with, so Oso told me that he would talk to his boss and try and get me in. Oso had his own oldie collection, so he played some of his gangster oldies—cool. Then in about a week, Oso called me and said it was all set up and to just come on down. Then he told me not to make him look bad. "Don't trip, brother. I'll work hard and do what the boss tells me." So now we saw each other at work and had our lunch together. He pulled out a photo and asked me what I thought. "Hey, she looks good, bro. Who is she?"

Then he said, "Here's the phone number. Call her and talk to her. They call her Gordy." Then he joked and said, "Do your thing, you big playa you."

The next day, I called her, and we had some small talk, and that was about it.

The next day at lunch, I called Gordy from work on my lunch break. "Hey, is Gordy there?"

"Yeah, hold on, let me get her."

Cool. Then Gordy got on the phone. "Hey, what's up, girl? How you doing? This is Chino. Remember me? We talked yesterday. Dave gave me your number so we might get to know each other."

She said, "Yeah, now I remember you, and it's cool if you want to talk."

"My name is William, but they call me Chino."

Then she said, "My name is Delia, but they call me Gordy."

We started to talk just a little while, then I told her that I got to get back to work, so we cut it short. "Hey, can I call you later?"

"Sure, that would be just fine, and you sure are good looking." She laughed. Then I got back to work.

Dave asked me, "So what happened, playa? How did it go?"

I said, "We just broke the ice. I'm not thinking too much ahead. I'll just see what might happen."

I was still seeing Renee and asked her if she wanted to take a ride to Patterson to visit my sons. She said, "Sure." Then I told her that we would be spending the night. "That's cool." So we took off to Patterson and got there. I got to play with my two sons, and Renee kept me company. We got our little drink on; we were all having a good time—not getting drunk, just a little buzzed. Monica's mom didn't mind me taking another female over her house—just as long as I stayed and gave my sons a good visit. Now it was getting late; we had already eaten dinner and were tired. So she gave us some blankets for bed. We slept in the living room. Well, Renee just slept in her little bra and sexy panties; I had some boxers. So we made love after the coast was clear. As we were sleeping, Renee kept taking off her blankets. All you could see was her sexy body, so I had to cover her up. She was a wild sleeper, shit I did not mind at all.

Then the next day, we got ready for breakfast. I played with my son Willie then played with Albert; we had a blast. As good as it was, we had to come back to San Jo so I could get back to work then get Renee back to her little son. Now we were back, and I dropped off Renee then got back home and told my tia that I just got back from seeing my sons.

"Good, mijo. How are they doing?"

"Good, Tia." I was happy that everything went as planned. I went to work the next day, and it was all good.

So now I was back at work and started to get at Gordy. I called her during my lunch breaks. We started to get along, but she didn't know how I looked. I already knew how she looked from the photo. I was just trying to get her attention and take it from there. We weren't getting too close, just talking about what she liked to do. Dave already told me that she liked to drink. I asked Gordy if she liked to listen to oldies. She said, "Heck yeah," so we had something in common.

It was getting close to Christmas and New Year's. I was thinking about Renee, and we spent New Year's together and had a good time.

Then Renee still had her main boyfriend, so I had to cut her loose. I didn't want to play myself to close. We still stayed friends. I wanted my own woman whom I didn't have to share with another man. Then I had to go to court for my son Albert in early January. As I was in court waiting to see what was going to happen with my son, here came Monica. She had her new boyfriend with her. Ms. Monica pulled me to the side and said that I could visit our son at her sister's house. So I followed them to the house, and we chilled out for just a little while. Out of nowhere, Monica asked me to give her a ride to the store, so we went. Then as I was driving, Monica pulled up her shirt and showed me her beautiful breast. *Whoa, baby.* Then she asked me if I wanted to go to Patterson with her for the weekend. I said, "What about your boyfriend?"

She said, "Don't trip."

So I said, "That sounds cool. Just let me stop at my house and get some money. Giddyap."

I was off to Patterson to visit my two sons just for a little while. Soon as we got to Patterson, we chilled out for about an hour, then we went to the room. I got some afternoon delight—cool. Then we played with our two sons and her daughter. We had a good time. I only stayed for the weekend then told Monica that I had to get back to San Jo to get to work. She was crying when I left, but what could I do? It was not going to work with us—just a booty call. She was set in her ways, and I was set in mine. So we tried to just stay friends from here on out. So now I was back to home base, San Jo. I now had to get back on track. I went to work and told Dave about my little wild weekend—that I got to visit my two sons and see the mother too. I had a good time.

Dave and I were talking at our lunch break, and he said, "What about Gordy?"

"Hey, she doesn't seem like she likes me much."

Then Dave told me, "You got to keep trying to get her attention."

So I called Gordy's house, and we started to talk. Now she sounded a little sexier as we talked, like flirting with me. Little by little, she was warming up to me. I would say she sure looked like an Aztec princess and how I would like her to listen to some oldies and chill out with me. I would play her some over the phone, and she said they sounded cool. So we were talking on the phone for about one week, then she said that I could go and give her a visit. She wanted to know just how I looked, so we made a date. I thought that she might like my style and what I was about. Then I called her after work, I got home, and she told me where to pick her up at. She said she wanted to chill with me, and I did want to chill with her. So now it was on. I met her at Twenty-Sixth and Julian. Man oh man, she looked even better in person. She had on some skintight pants and a sexy blouse. "Hey, Gordy, what's up? You look so cool." Then I asked her what she wanted to do.

"Let's go to the park and chill out there."

"All right." Then I opened the door for her and let her sit down. "Giddyap. Monte, let's go."

Now I put on some oldies, and she said, "Play that one again. I like it."

I could sense that she was feeling more at ease with me; that was good. I was not trying to come on to strong, but she looked so sexy, I just wanted to take her in my arms. Our first date went just fine. I did not even get a good night kiss, but that was all right. We still had our little talks during my lunch breaks, and I went to visit Gordy more and more, and she finally gave me that precious kiss. We started to hang out more. "Let me take you out for dinner." Then I asked her if she wanted to go to the drive-in, Capitol. So I asked Gordy if she would spend the night with me after the movies.

She said, "Let's see what happens, and we will take it from there."

That sounded good. So it was Friday night. I went to pick up Gordy from her house, and we stopped and got some tacos and got a six-pack of Coronas for the movies. She wanted to see that movie *The Bodyguard* with Whitney Houston; that was cool with me. Hey, I was feeling lucky; this might be the night.

Now we were both watching this movie, drinking a Corona, with Gordy at my side, and she was looking super fine. She had on a lace top and some skintight black pants then that makeup, looking like a northern star, classy lady. So we finished drinking the six-pack of Coronas, and the movie was now over. I was good to go. First, I asked Gordy, "So what's it gonna be? You spending the night, or do I drive you home?"

Then she said, "No, I'll stay with you tonight."

Cool. Shit, I couldn't get home fast enough. I started to keep my cool and take it easy on the way home. So we pulled up at the house, and we got down from the car. I was licking my lips, feeling like the big bad wolf. We got inside my bedroom and got cozy. I put on some oldies, turned down the lights, and tried to set the mood. Gordy got under the covers first and told me to pull down her tight pants. "No problem." I sure was glad that I did work out; I had to use all my strength to pull off her puppies. Then I got into my boxers and took off my shirt, and off to heaven I went. We started to make out, skin on skin; she was super soft and silky. Then it was getting pretty hot under the covers—if you know what I mean, Jack. Now it was time to pull off her sexy little silky panties. "Whoa. Gordy, are you ready for me? You had me waiting for a while, baby doll." So I got out on my boxers and started to handle my business. She felt like a virgin. Whoa, boy, after about five minutes, I busted one, and it was a big load. My freakin' toes curled, that's for sure. I hoped that hers did too. Then I told Gordy, "I ain't finished with you yet, understand, baby doll?" It was the best sex that I ever had, and that's the truth. After that, we both went to bed and called it a good night. I was feeling like a million bucks after two nuts. My whole body was feeling so good; like a hand in a glove was the way our bodies joined. Gordy was just a little shy at first then was like a tiger in the bedroom. I guess you could say that I made the freak come out to play. Talk about feeling like a northern Aztec king. I was him, and he was me.

The next morning, we got up from sleeping. "How did you sleep, Gordy?"

"Cool, but something kept poking me last night."

"Is that right? I wonder."

She was not hating it one bit. She put on this sexy smile, and the way she moaned.

So we both woke up with a smile on our faces, then we got washed up. Hey, that loving was worth the wait. It released both our sexual tension—at least mine. Then my other tia (Nellie) asked me to do her a favor. She wanted me to give her new boyfriend a ride back to his house. "No problem. Just let us get ready, and I'll take him wherever he needs to go." So everybody was ready. "Giddyap, let's go." First, I dropped off Gordy. She gave me a nice, long French kiss bye. Then she told me thanks for letting her spend the night with me. She said that she was warm all over all through the night. It was like a dream to me at the time, too good to be happening to me. She was so pretty and sexy; how could I be so blessed? So now I gave my tia's boyfriend his ride to his house. He gave me a $20 for my gas and troubles. I thanked him for his love and support.

Gordy called me later on, so we talked. I asked her, "So how did you like our first night together?" She said that she couldn't complain. Hey, I did not want her to feel ashamed that we made love together. I would just play it as it came and wouldn't get my hopes up to high. So I said a prayer to our Lord: "Please let this beautiful woman fall for me—even just for a little while. Amen." So we were getting to know each other more and more. Gordy was telling me that she wanted to change her way of living on the fast lane. Hey, I did understand this; all that being locked up—there was no future in that. She seemed to open up to me some of her goals and dreams and other things and of doing the right things instead of doing the wrong things in this life. Yeah, we must learn from our parents' mistakes as well as our own mistakes. I could feel a little bit that I was growing on her, and she was growing on me too. I didn't want to come on too strong. I wanted to take it slow and just let this love affair grow. We started to see each other more and got closer.

I was still working with my friend, Dave. Then I put this job application for this place called Glassforms. This job was just up the street from where I was working. Well, Glassforms called me, and I turned them down. I was loyal to the work that I already had—no hard feelings. So I went to work with Dave; we talked at our lunch breaks. He asked how everything with me and Gordy was.

"Well, it's going smooth, brother." Then I told Dave, "Hey, check this out. This other company called me about work. I shot them down. I wanted a for-sure thing, *tu sabes* (understand), brother?"

"Yeah, stay here with me and learn this tool and die, program, cool." Then Dave asked me, "Why don't you and your new lady, Gordy, come over for some dinner?"

"Hey, sounds good. Let me ask Gordy. See what she says. Then I'll get back to you, Dave."

Well, lunch was over. It was time to get back to work; the party was over. Sometimes I'd really feel that with the little brother that I lost when I was seventeen years old, now I had been blessed with my friend, brother Dave (Oso). Then I asked Gordy, "What about dinner with Dave and his lady?" She said that would be just fine. So we went to dinner with Dave and his family. First, he and I drank a brew, and so did the ladies. I made two toasts—first one to my little brother then to all the fallen northern Aztec Warriors. Then we ate. Right after dinner, we chilled out and drank some more, and Dave put on his gangster oldies. We were all having a good time, and it was mellow. Now it was starting to get late, so we left, and Gordy was letting me spend the night more and more. Now I was really starting to feel that this was real, with me and Gordy. When we would make love, I felt time just stood still, you feel me? Then I was really feeling like a northern Aztec king, and Gordy was my northern Azteca queen. This newfound ecstasy was so real to me, my own Playboy Bunny. Man oh man, when I came, a chill went all up my spine from head to toe; I could feel it. I was on top of the world. Then in public, all the men would check out my queen, stuck on. "Stupid, snap out of it." Thank you, Lord, for bringing her into my world, this beautiful baby girl. Let me tell you, hey, you know how beautiful and sexy Ms. Jennifer Lopez is? Gordy looks just like her, like a twin. That's a hot to trot with that bedroom body. Men dream about females like that, while I had Ms. Gordy on mine. So when we made love, all I wanted to do was satisfy her in the lovemaking department, you know what I mean? I felt almost like Gordy was some kind of movie star here in San Jo, and lucky me, I got to make love to her, yeah, yeah.

My friend and I stayed working for a while, then I got the axe and got laid off; work got really slow. Then I started to collect unemployment checks till I found some more work. Yeah, now Gordy and I were a couple. Gordy and her brother with his lady got this apartment on Tenth and Santa Clara, so I helped them move into their new place. Then Gordy asked me if I wanted to move in with her and her six-year-old son. I made up my mind right away. "Let me just tell my tia and get my stuff." It really felt too good to be true, like some kind of fairy tale or something. How could this beautiful queen fall for a guy like me? First, you must get the money then the power, and only then do you get the beautiful princess. Hey, I'd take the dream girl, and then I'd get the money, like *Scarface*, then power. I was just going to enjoy this as long as I could.

So we were chilling out in the pool; whoa, what a good way to beat the heat. God had blessed me, that's for sure. Well, Gordy had on a two-piece bikini, and I just had my cutoffs, and I was still in pretty good shape myself. Being around Gordy did make me feel sexy; she sure was sexy. All the men in the pool could not stop staring at her; hey, she was like a movie star in the flesh. Then after our little swim, we would take our little shower shots—oh boy, that was the best. She was made just for me, and I was made for her—like a hand in a glove *when we made love.*

I still had to report to my probation officer, get over there, and do what I got to do—like give them a bottle then start going to domestic violence classes then NA classes. "Are you working?" I told them that I was just laid off my last job and I was looking for work and that once I did find some, I would report back. He told me to come back in two weeks. "All right then, you have a good day." We took off back to the house. Then I let Gordy know that I had been physical with Monica. She never said anything more about the subject. Then I told her that I also had two sons from Monica. So now we got back to home base, and I got about a dime bag of smoke. I asked Gordy's primo if he wanted to help me get my smoke on. "After this, I'm stopping cold turkey." We were getting our little drink on that night. Then Gordy started having a fit about Monica's name on my chest.

Gordy was having this big old fit. "You better get her name covered up, like yesterday."

"Check this out, baby doll. Let me call my homeboy." I made the call. "Hey, Caveman, I need this big favor."

He said, "So what's up, Chino?"

"I do need some artwork done."

Caveman said, "Come on down. Shop's open just for you, bro."

"I'm on my way, baby boy." I got ready and left in the Monte, and I got to his house. I knocked; he let me in.

"So what's the problem?"

"Hey, Caveman, I got my new baby doll, Gordy, and still have my ex lady's name right on my chest."

He told me not to worry. "Let's just put some roses and a humming bird and that butterfly there. Hey, you will never know the difference."

"That sounds cool."

"Let's get started. Come out of your shirt. Now let's get to work, brother of mine." So Caveman got his tattoo gun with his Indian ink and started to get busy. "Check it out, Chino. Gordy will never have anything to say."

I told Caveman, "Thanks. So what do I owe you?"

"This one is on the strength, carnal (brother). Let's just say this is my gift to you, Chino. Don't you trip."

"All right, when I come up with more cash flow, I'd want some more work done."

"No problem. For sure."

So I left, gave Caveman that gangster hug, and got back to my house. First, I went inside and woke up Gordy. "Get up, my sweet darling, and check it out."

Gordy was happy, and she told me to come to bed and gave me some good loving. She was a tiger, and she told me how happy she was now. "Now you belong to me, and I belong to you. Now we are bonding real nice."

After about two months, we found a larger apartment at her mother's apartments. This was cool, and this new apartment was cleaner and bigger, so we were all happy. Then this one morning, Gordy said this wasn't working and that I needed to find some work.

"All right, babe, I'll go out today and see what I can find." I went to that Glassforms company and filled out another job application. They gave me this math test then some stuff with the ruler, and I passed the test. Then they sent me out for a drug test, and I passed. So they hired me in about two days; that was cool. They told me that I would be working swing shift from three thirty till eleven thirty; that was all right with me. That was way better than graveyard. First, they got me boxing items of fiberglass. Then one of my coworkers got me on machines. So now I got on one these fiberglass machines; he told me to look for this and that. I got it. Then he came back, and machines were running smooth. His name was Ernie, then he told our boss, "Hey, Will wants to train on the machines."

"All right then, Will, we will get you started first chance we get."

So I went back to boxing and called it a night. After a while, Gordy wanted me to be the father of her next child. Oh, that would be beautiful; we would have a love child. I had two sons already, then she had her son, Julian. We said maybe a beautiful little daughter. So Gordy told me, "Let's go to the bedroom. I'm ovulating right now."

"Hey, you're the boss, my love."

So our sex was blessed to the fullest that this was no one-night stand. Now she was giving me sex with that sexy smile and the way she moaned in a sexy way.

Now she said that she was pregnant; alrighty then, my boys were working good. One night, I got home from work, and Gordy was crying in the room. "What's the matter with my sexy baby doll?" She hugged me and told me that she just lost the baby. So I just wiped away her tears and held mine inside; we fell asleep in each other's arms. That was bittersweet. We took it in stride, and I tried to cheer Gordy up, my angel. We went to the movies, got a fancy dinner, and the works. For I was busting ass at work, making a little more cash. Then I was learning more and more how these damn machines worked—the dos and the don'ts, the setups, and the tear-downs of the machines. We were renting movies, getting pizzas, and living the fairy tale life. I started going to these drug meetings and going to my domestic violence classes. My baby doll looked more lovely with each day that passed. Hey, I ain't even lying, I felt like I was in a dream; sometimes, after we would make love, I had to pinch myself just to make sure that I was not just dreaming. Hey, I was like a northern Aztec king, and Gordy was my queen.

Well, after about a month, I got home from work, and Gordy was waiting up for me. "Oh, you're home. How was your shift, babe?"

"Went by all right."

Then Gordy said, "Chino, I'm ready to try again. I'm just starting to ovulate." Then she said, "Come to the room, you big brute." Then Gordy told me, "Chino, you come here and make me have your baby girl."

So now I got to rock her world. First, I told Gordy, "Hey, I ain't trying to hurt you down there. Are you sure that you're ready?" We went into the bedroom and began to get our freak on. I busted one after about five minutes, and Gordy told me she wasn't done with me yet. So I was reloading, getting ready for some more. The first one doesn't count; besides, the second nut is always better anyways, *que no*? So I was putting in work under the sheets, and when a fine baby doll wants to get pregnant, the sex is great. Give it to your sexy mama. Man, I went to heaven that night, that's for sure. Now Gordy was being sexy as she could be with me; that was cool. Then in about a month, Gordy was waking up with morning sickness.

"You got me pregnant, you bastard. Just kidding." Gordy liked being pregnant; just that morning sickness, she could do without. So we both hugged, and I made breakfast, for us. Then I got ready to go to work. I was on cloud nine, just knowing that she let me get her pregnant and she wanted my baby. This would keep us bonded for life even if things didn't work out in the long run. Gordy made me feel like a million bucks, priceless, walking on air. Then I finished my classes and got off probation—cool. I was making all the right moves and going to a steady job, and to top it off, I got a sexy lady at my side. So now I kept going to work, doing the best job that I could, and learning something new every day. Then I started to make more money; I was taking home about $250 per week. Back in 1993, that was not too bad, better than minimum wage, that's for sure. I got my car all taken care of, like the tags and then car insurance; everything was going our way. Gordy was starting to get bigger and bigger now that she was about four months pregnant. Gordy still looked very sexy even being pregnant, I must say, and the sex was to die for. She was a tiger, let me tell you, tearing me up. So I had to take Gordy to prenatal care, which was cool, to see how our baby was doing. Gordy had just made me a happy and proud man, like I had my very own throne and a crown. I knew now we would be bonded for life in the best way because of our baby.

After about eight months on swing shift, now I began to work day shift, which was seven thirty till three thirty, then I got to the house by four thirty—right on time for dinner. I could take Gordy to all her doctor's appointments. Sometimes at work, my so-called coworkers would say, "Hey, Will, your lady's here."

I said, "I can see your eyes popping out of your eye sockets."

But they were still trying to give me my respect. "How did you pull that sexy babe, Chino?"

"Hey, I can't call it. Maybe she likes the way I tuck her bed at night. She must like my style, even for just a little while."

"Brother, whoa, a true northern Azteca princess in the flesh."

Sometimes Gordy would say, "Why do they look at me when I come to pick you up from work, babe?"

"Hey, Gordy, you are very beautiful, like you don't like the attention, brat. That's why I chose you, for I love everything about you, Gordy."

At my dear job, I had three kick-overs; that meant the resin got to warm then got hot. It turned like smoke and lava, then it was all bad. Well, that had happened to me three times, and I was hot myself. Then I turned it into something positive, a learning experience. When that happened, it put you all behind on everything. I made the best of it and moved on to the next job. Now you must work harder, faster, and better the next time around. Then I met this one brother from my neighborhood; his name was Sly. He said, "Ain't you the brother of that little boy who got killed at Mayfair Park?"

"Yeah, that would be me."

"Hey, what's up, brother?"

I had known that he had been to the joint too in the past. We were all just trying to make a nice, fresh start and work for a living. So we talked about the job, overall just shop talk. We would take our little lunch breaks together and bullshit. We got our little smoke on after we ate our dinner and sometimes listened to some oldies too. Then one day, Sly hit me up, "Hey, how long are you gonna mourn for your little brother?" I didn't have anything to say at the time. I had got stuck and had no comeback.

Well, the next day, I talked to Sly and told him, "Till the day that *I die*. For every breath I take, every push-up that I do, every nut that I bust, every dollar that I make, that's also for my little brother."

Then Sly said, "That's a good way of looking at it, Chino."

So now we were on the same page, now working at a good, solid company with good benefits.

Hey, almost half the work crew were all ex-convicts, just right out the penitentiary and just trying to get back on track. I stayed in pretty good shape, working out at the house after work. Gordy would ask me, "Babe, why are you so committed to working out?"

I said, "My love, I say a prayer for my dead brother then for the fallen northern Aztec warriors and for you, Gordy. That you feel me strong when we make love and when our bodies touch. Then if I'm ready to fight, it won't be a problem. With these men at my work, it's on at the drop of a hat."

One day, when I first started working at Glassforms, this one guy just kept looking at me like I had stolen something. So I saw him outside at break time. "What's up, bro?" Do you know me? Well, here's my name: William Navarro Ruiz. They call me Chino from the eastside of San Jo, baby boy."

"Hey, Will, it's all good. I'm here to make that money. That's it. Let's be nice and get some of this green."

I made this guy think about looking at me funny again. See, my friend Sly knew that I knew how to do that northern Aztec dance. That meant that I had a reputation for knowing how to use my hands and feet in battle, so we always demanded the utmost respect— almost like an image to uphold. Stay strong in the body and be true to this. Well, our company had this picnic at great America, so Gordy and I went with her son to have a good time. We had stayed all day, getting on all the rides. We saw a couple of my coworkers there, and we talked. I had introduced them to my Gordy and her son, Julian. "How you doing?"

"No, how you doing?"

"We just trying to enjoy this beautiful day here."

Then they told me, "Hey, your lady is starting to show."

"Yah, she's about five months pregnant." Then we went about our day. "Take care, brother. See you at work." It was starting to get dark, and I asked Julian if he was ready to go.

"Yeah, let's get back to the house and call it a day."

"Let's giddyap and go." My little *familia* had a good time. When we got home, I asked, "Hey, Julian, how did you love that?"

"I loved it, Chino. Thanks a lot." Then he said, "Thanks for the company too. Man, Chino, those guys whom you work with, they all look like gangster status—yeah, like you."

"Yeah, we come from the same background in a way, but they are good."

Then Julian and I had a little talk man-to-man. Julian was about six years old. "Hey, listen, mijo, I know that you really don't like sharing your mother with me. I'm not trying to steal your mother away from you, and I ain't trying to take the place of your father." I told Julian that I had two sons of my own. We would go to Patterson to visit them once every two months, so Julian had already known that I had my two sons—just that we were not that close. Then I told him not to be afraid of me and that I would never put hands on him or his beloved mother, Gordy. So Julian and I made the best out of this little situation. We had this understanding in a good way. We never got too close, me and Julian.

One day, we were chilling out with one of Gordy's homegirls and her old man. They had a small barbecue, and we went to have a good time. We were drinking some brew and playing with the kids. Then we all went inside and listened to some oldies, still drinking and playing some cards. Her old man was holding the bag of PCP, selling on the block. As we were still drinking, he started to talk shit about my friend Dave (Oso) and disrespected him. I didn't like that shit, so I told him, "Save all that melodrama for somebody else, bro." Then I told Gordy that it was time to go and leave this place.

Then Gordy said, "Chino, why you got to make trouble when I bring you."

So I told her just what had happened and what he said, then she agreed with me. "I ain't no two-faced, and I don't smoke that shit anyways." I was still smoking weed, and that was about it. I just told homeboy, "When you see Dave, handle your business." He was speechless, got stuck on stupid or something. We just went home, then the next day, I called my friend and told him to stay on his toes. "Hey, Dave, I seen your homeboy last night."

"Who?"

"Huero."

"Is that right, Chino?"

"Yeah, he was talking out the side of his neck about you, bro. Hey, don't worry, I was checking him out. He's soft, the booze and the coochie. All right, you take care, Dave, and keep your head up."

"Loyalty above all odds, brother. Forget that little joker. I got bigger and better things to worry about."

The next day, they called to talk to Gordy and asked me if I had a problem. "It's all good. Don't trip. I said what I had to say last night. Kill game."

Yeah, I was still a little heated, so the next time that I worked out, I was thinking about this fool. It made me work out harder and with more anger, feeling stronger. Gordy knew that I was getting busy when I did have to sling these sharks. She told me that it made her feel sexy inside and that it turned her on right after I finished my little workout. Gordy would say, "Bring it to mama. Let me feel you, daddy, nice and tight." Then we would take our sexy little shower; man oh man, that was great, baby. Now we were just like a team, and I was the coach. Gordy got back to the program and was giving me love up and down, whoa.

At work, they were having another family picnic at Raging Waters, so we went to have a good time and let Julian have his fun. It was a really big company picnic, then they got the Employee of the Month. So they started calling out names, and what would you know, I won. They gave you a certificate plus $100. Well, soon as I got back to Gordy, she took the money and said it was for the love child—cool. I felt real nice having my beautiful queen at my side, like I was just floating on air. But this was way too real, and it was. All I could hear was "Congratulations, bro, and keep up the good work." So we were happy, and it was starting to get dark. Her son had a good time, getting wet on all the rides. So finally, we had all our fun in the sun and left back home.

It was already time for my vacation, but I put it on hold. I was just waiting for Gordy to have our baby. So now we were on August 11, 1994, and God bless that day. I went to work and got home after work. Then Gordy wanted to go to her mother's house, so we went. We chilled out there for a while. We ate dinner and played that waiting game. I posted up, just waiting for Gordy to tell me that her water broke. Well, after about an hour, it broke, so I took Gordy with her mother to the hospital. We got there, and they gave us a room to see if she was ready to have the baby. The doctor told her, "Not just yet. Go back home." So we got back to her mother's house and waited. I knew that tonight was the night; we just had to wait a little bit longer.

Then Gordy was crying and said, "Take me back to the hospital."

So here we went again, back to the hospital, then they sent her home again. We got back to her mom's.

CHAPTER 9

MINE AND GORDY'S FIRST DAUGHTER, DESTINY

Hey, they say that the third time is a charm. Now we were back at the house of Gordy's mother. So we relaxed and chilled out for about an hour, then Gordy said, "This time, it's for real." I took her mother with us for support. *Bam*, right when we got to the hospital, we went straight into the delivery room. I stayed outside the room; I did not want Gordy to feel embarrassed. I went right on in after she had our daughter Destiny's birth. Destiny's nose was pushed back. Gordy said, "Chino daddy, look at our new baby girl." It made me proud.

"Gordy, you did good, Mama. Now you get your rest, my love. I love you for this, Gordy." When she was in labor, all she was saying was "You bastard Chino." Then "I hate you, Chino." Well, Gordy asked the doctor to put two stitches down there for Chino; how nice was that?

The next day, I went to pick up both my bundles of joy. We had our first beautiful daughter together. I was a blessed man; yes, I was. Then I called my work and told them that my lady just had the baby. That was when I got my one-week vacation. "Congratulations, Mr. Ruiz."

Thanks, I'll be there next week."

"Enjoy. See you when you come back to work."

Now we were taking care of our new little angel; Destiny started to look more and more beautiful with each passing day. Gordy was happy that it was all over with—no stretch marks. So Gordy could still look so sexy; she still had a sexy, precious bedroom body. That one-week vacation just went by so fast; I went back to work. After about a month, Gordy took our Destiny to my work, and they all loved her; she was so pretty. Then we called her a Glassforms baby girl. I was on top of my world, for sure. Everything was going my way; I thanked our Lord for all his blessings. Then I was getting more oldies to add to my collection. Now we were going shopping for new baby bottles, diapers, and other things—baby swing and that baby stroller. Gordy still had some baby stuff from the baby shower they threw for her. We would go to the flea market to get some other goodies for the apartment. At the flea market, they had this oldie shop that had all those hard-to-find oldies, so there I would be, checking and buying some tapes. We all had a good time; Julian would get his little goodies, toys, and other things. Every Friday, we all went to eat out—nothing big, just Taco Bell.

Then we would go to the movies or rent some movies. We always had something going on. It was lovely. After that, Gordy still had her sexy bedroom body back; hey, I was not hating that. Now they got that profit sharing at work plus them other stuff. On payday, they gave me a $1,000 check for all the good hard work that I had been doing. So when I got home, I told Gordy. Then we split up the money, $500 for me and $500 for Gordy. I got my new car gear, some more speakers, and new car stereo; then I had some more money left over. Gordy went to party with her homegirls and got some sexy new outfits, like some teddy bears, then with her hair in ponytails. Whoa, she looked so sexy when she wore them; I was living my dream.

Well, now little Destiny was about three months old when I got this phone call at my work. Gordy just got busted, and she was in the jailhouse. They had arrested hair for drunk driving plus some other stuff. Her brother brought my Monte to my job and filled me in on what was really going on. "Yeah, Chino, my sister got pulled over and told the officer, 'Please don't tow my boyfriend's car away, please.' So they just parked my Monte and took her away." Could you blame the officer? Here was this beautiful Latina just crying her eyes out. Then we went to the house of Gordy's mother, just waiting for her to call. Gordy called about an hour later, and they gave me the phone.

"Hello, Gordy, what happened?" Then she told me that she was drinking with some of her friends, then they got pulled over. They got her for being high on that PCP, and she would know more after she went to court. Gordy was telling me how sorry she was then that she loved me. So I told Gordy not to worry and that I would be there for her. "I'm here for you, my baby doll. I'll take care of you, send you money, and visit you." Gordy knew that she had to be there for a while. "Just stay strong, my love. Hey, once you get back, we will make up for all this lost time." Now my world got all turned upside down for a while. On the weekends, I would take Julian and Destiny to visit Gordy; that made both our days.

"I'll make it greater later."

"I know that you will, Gordy." I was lucky that I had some of Gordy's family helping me.

So while Gordy was locked up, we were sending each other love letters in the mail. Then I sent her that money that she needed. Lucky for me, I got the old lady of Gordy's brother babysitting for me. She took care of Julian and Destiny during the week. Then on the weekends, I would pick them up. It kept me pretty busy. I worked all week, then on Friday nights, I'd go pick up Julian and Destiny. First, we got something to eat. Then we went to rent some movies and chill out at our apartment. It was very small but cozy. We would stay up late, me and Julian, putting Destiny to sleep. He was my right-hand man—in a good way. Hey, almost everybody thinks that their kids are the prettiest baby in town. Well, when you would see little Destiny, you could not help but fall in love with how beautiful she was. Really, this was the truth; her grandmother loved her too much—and all the girls in the family. Destiny was a bundle of joy, that's for sure.

Gordy would get her visits early Saturday mornings. So Julian and I had to get up early to make sure that we made Gordy's visits. This would make Gordy's morning, that's for sure. Then they gave us contact visits; we got to hug and two kisses. Gordy would be happy just for a little while. It made me sick to leave her in that place, but you'd play, you'd pay. I got those hugs and kisses; I loved those contact visits. Now Gordy's time was going by pretty fast. She was getting shorter and shorter to the house. Then we could be a good, happy family once again. So as our visit was over, I got to hold her and give her a long kiss. I told her, "Everything is gonna be all right. I'm taking care of the fort. Put your trust in me, my baby. I'm not cheating on you out here." I stayed true to Gordy and myself.

One day, while I was waiting for my visit with Gordy, I was playing this gangster rap loudly. The guard told me to lower my music, so I did—no problem. Sometimes during our little visits, Gordy would give me a little tita shot; that was cool. *Just be good, Chino.* I knew that it would be worth waiting for that good old Gordy loving. I just made the best out of the situation at hand and just took one day at a time. While at work, they wanted the day shift to switch with graveyard for a two-week period. Hey, what could you do but just go with the program? I really didn't care; Gordy was still busted.

My new shift was from midnight to seven thirty in the morning. So I was trying it outlet so bad, then my lady was not home right now. She was still in jail, but she was getting short to the house. Then the second week, early in the morning, I was fast asleep. When all of a sudden, my Gordy woke me up, wearing a sexy teddy. "Hi, babe. I'm out, big daddy. Make love to me already." I thought that I was still in a dream, but it was way too real. "Oh, how I missed you, and I want to feel you inside of me." So we made love, and it was beautiful. Gordy was hungry for me, and I was hungry for her. Then the first one didn't count, just a warm-up. Then we chilled out for a while, then we made some more love. "I'm going to tear you up," she told me. "Handle your business."

Gordy was talking nasty to me, so I started talking nasty to her too. "Whose kitty cat is this?"

"Yours, big daddy."

We went to heaven, and it was like time just had stopped for both of us. First, you got that makeup sex, then you got that get-me-pregnant sex. Then you got that sex just to have sex, then you got that just-got-out-of-jail sex. They were all cool—better when it was happening to you. So I busted my second nut, and Gordy was not done with me. Gordy's kitty cat was meow-meowing, then I had it purring, and she was feeling just fine. I had to say to Gordy, "You been a bad girl. Now I have to give you a spanking." She agreed with me. "You got fire in between those sexy thighs, and I will put out that fire with some warm milk." Whoa, we made up for lost time, that's for sure. It blew my mind; making love to Gordy was superfine. It was good to have my Gordy back home with our Destiny and Julian.

Now it was time for me to go back to work—with a big smile and love bites on my neck. My coworkers knew that my lady was out and were happy for me. So now after work, I got to come home to my lady and my Destiny and Julian. Destiny was looking more beautiful with each passing day, more like her pretty mama. Gordy was acting sweeter now, and it felt like this would last forever. Plus doing those sixty days maybe made her think two times of how she'd act now. Like *I'm really gonna be good when I get back out and be true to myself just for a little while.* We were getting along just fine, and I was back on day shift.

Gordy was grateful to me for making her feel like a woman once again. No more whacking the pud; she had me feeling like a stud. My daughter and I were getting closer, for I was playing mommy and daddy for two months. Hey, that was love—taking care of our little angel, like changing her when she needed to and rocking her in my arms to sleep. Thank you, God, for this beautiful blessing. Destiny was so soft and pure, that's for sure. I always told myself that little warrior sons made their fathers strong, but little girls made their fathers much stronger. For now I would and must protect Destiny from any harm then let it be known that her daddy was a strong northern Aztec warrior. This way, people would think twice before even thinking of harming my beloved only *mija* (daughter). Some of the nights when Gordy was still locked up, Destiny would just cry and cry till she fell asleep on my shoulder. Well, that was then; the good times were here again. Gordy always showed our daughter off to her family and her girlfriends then let them know that I was a very proud daddy with her devilish, sexy smile.

We got together with one of her girlfriends. Then I had known her old man, Tony, from when we were little guys. Plus about one year before, he had put some tattoos on me. The "smile now, cry later" faces came out cool. So Gordy wanted to chill with them—no problem. We got some brew and chips. "Hey, what's up, Tony? Here's the Coronas, and our ladies can chop it up." We started to get our little drink on; Tony and I went outside to smoke a joint. Then I hit up Tony, "You still got your tattoo gun, and you still slanging that ink?"

"Hey, Chino, you know that I always need that tax-free Sunday money, baby boy."

"Well, check this out. I want my Destiny's name, then I want Gordy's name on the back of my neck."

"Yeah, we can do that. Let me go get my tattoo gun, and we will get busy, brother."

"Hey, then put *forever mine* under Gordy's name."

"No problem. Don't you worry, Chino. I'll fix you right up. First, we do your daughter's name, then well do Gordy's with *forever mine*. That will be your crown that you wear to let people know that Gordy is your northern Azteca queen. This shall be my gift to you, brother. No charge, Chino." Tony said, "This is a token of our long friendship."

"Hey, that's cool. How's it coming out?"

"Clean. You are gonna love it when I'm done. Here's the mirror, Chino. Just check it out."

"All right, Tony, you got that magic touch, for sure. Now let's clean it up and start on another Corona."

We were having a good time, and our ladies were still making up for lost time. Good job. It started to get dark, and we asked Tony and his lady, "Maybe next week, you can chill out at our little apartment." They said yes. "Hey, we will rent some movies and get our little drink on and break bread. Then we can listen to some gangster oldies."

"Sounds like a plan."

Hey, I would rather chill with Tony instead of that other sidebuster. I could trust him around my Gordy and my daughter. I didn't have to watch my back all the time. Then we went a ways back, me and Tony, like true brothers. That night, after we got home, we made love like animal attractions, whoa, all in a blessed way. She took me all inside of her, and she was so horny, I took all that I could get. Hey, when you are blessed with a sexy female, you always begin to wonder when she will stop being in love with you and when will she get tired of you and find somebody brand-new. Then you gotta be on top of your game always, like Romeo. Always be at your best behavior and never get upset. Gordy played off her beauty, and that was just fine. She could be with any man, but she chose me. Thank the Lord for that; she was my sexy brat. Whenever we went somewhere, all eyes were on her always—like she lit up the room with her sexy bedroom body. When we went out to the fair, all the men could not stop staring at her; it made me mad. Hey, they could only look; she was with me and was my lady. *Go ahead and look all you want. I get to take her home with me, baby boys.* Sometimes Gordy didn't like it when they just kept looking, but she looked so fine, they couldn't help it. Gordy would giggle and say "You get to rape me, and I get to rape you, Chino" in a good, sexy way. Well, we would take our little family photos at the fair, so we had to look good. They always came out pretty clean. We had our little family unit. Don't get me wrong, I worshipped the ground Gordy walked on, that's for sure. She was my love goddess, like a fairy tale.

Northern Aztec warrior got blessed with a beautiful northern Azteca princess as a precious gift for me losing my little brother. Our Lord had blessed me with Ms. Gordy. Still, life could be very beautiful. It helped me fill this void in my heart for my little bro. Thank you, Lord, and I shall enjoy this blessing as long as I could. Gordy would have to do the leaving me, for making love to Gordy was pure ecstasy. Something in my heart just could not bear to leave Gordy and our Destiny. As of now, we were still having fun, going here and there. We were living all together happily. Our little Destiny was starting to crawl, rolling over, and taking baby steps. Destiny was also starting to talk, like saying "Dada" and "Mama." Hey, it sounded lovely to me and Gordy. "Listen to your daughter saying this and that." I feel with most couples, after lovemaking, everything feels much better. Well, I knew that it did for me. I felt like a king or something—a million-dollar feeling. Everything was just about perfect—Like Adam and Eve in God's little paradise.

I was working days. I got to be with my little *familia* during the evening hours. It was so nice to eat our dinner then have Gordy for dessert. We were getting some overtime at work, which was another four hours. *Hey, bring it on then.* And ain't nobody special; everyone got their turn on the overtime. I would do my overtime in the first part of the week. Then when it was Friday, I would be off the hook. So on Friday nights, I would be with my little family unit. Now it was time for another income tax check; we split the money. I was going to get my car painted. Gordy wanted to party with all her girlfriends. We were still keeping all the family unit happy and going to birthday parties and the movies. I was finally getting my Monte painted. It was taking more time than I thought. Leaving my Gordy at home alone, I got caught up in the paint job, and Gordy started to smoke more and more of that PCP. She was just losing her mind on that stuff. One day after work, I got home, and she was all high on that stuff, so I got Destiny and Julian and went to the house of Gordy's mother till she came down. Then Gordy called the police on me. When the police got there, they arrested Gordy for being high and put her in jail. It backfired on her; she called me later, saying, "I'm sorry, babe. This time, I learned my lesson. Listen to me, Chino. When I get out, I'm gonna be your love slave—in a good way, baby boy."

So I did forgive her and sent her some money. Then I went to visit her with Julian and Destiny. I sent her some love letters to pass the time. Then I got my Monte back with a nice paint job, a nice maroon color. It made the Monte look so clean and mean. It had three coats of clear; I paid another $200 to wet-sand it. We made the best out of the situation, with Gordy being in jail. She acted different when she was locked up. "It's all about me and you." Now I was blind with love and went for anything she promised and said to me. What a sucker I was, and this was true. Hey, it all seemed worth it when she was in my arms—then her filling me with all her charms. I just felt that if our daughter had her real mother and father, Destiny was rich. I tried to be more forgiving to Gordy even when she would be ugly with me at times. Let's put it like this: when she was bad, she was very bad. Then when she was good, she was very good. She would take all my pain away and take me to heaven when we made love. She knew just what to say to make me feel like a king. After we made love, it was like fireworks, for sure; it was priceless. I had mad love for this mother of my *mija* (daughter).

When she was doing her time, I got caught for drunk driving, coming home from drinking with homeboy. They towed my car away. I got taken to jail and stayed till got bailed out. I was just lucky that I had a good boss. Then they helped me get my car out, and I still had to go to court. I got a lawyer who got me a hundred days due to a prior conviction—plus two hundred hours of community service. So now I got a break and got to keep my job. I still had to do time in the near future, just before I got hit up for back child support. Now the county was taking half my check, so I lost my little apartment. Then I moved in with my father here in San Jo.

Gordy finally got out, and I went to pick her up and took her to her mother's house. We went straight to the bedroom and got our little freak on. It was like being taken to heaven once again. Then we went at it again; she was a tiger. Gordy was like a ray of sunshine, and she was mine oh mine. Well, everything was going good for just a while. Gordy wanted to stay at her mother's house. Then while I was at my father's small trailer, I got a phone call from Gordy. She wanted me to go and get her, telling me she wanted to stay with me. Right before that, I was lying down, thinking about her and my Destiny and Julian. So I went and picked her up with Julian and Destiny. I brought them back to the small trailer. Then we started to get situated in this small space. I thanked our Lord; I cried on the inside—in a good way. Gordy and I were back together once again with our little family. We went to get something to eat then watched a little TV and got ready for bed. Well, Gordy let me get some tender loving. That made my night; we slept tight. Then early in the morning, before I went to work, she gave me some more loving. The week went by, and it was Friday already. So my coworkers and I got a six-pack and drank after work. I had about two beers, then I went home. Soon as I got back home, Gordy started a little fight with me for drinking. She just wanted to get back to her mother's house so she could party and smoke that PCP. So I let her go and do her thing.

Man oh man, my world just turned upside down once again. So I went and moved in with my sister for a little while before I had to do my hundred days myself. Gordy's party was nonstop. She was off the hook; she started smoking that meth with PCP. All that I could do was just stand by and watch her destroy herself. I was still going to work, and I would pass the house of Gordy's mother on the way and see who she was messing with. I also let her know that I was still around if she needed me. Gordy would let me have my Destiny and Julian for the weekends. Well, I was getting close to turning myself into jail, so I stopped going to work; I didn't want to get arrested right at work. I was getting myself good and ready to do this time. I got some news that my little son Albert was very sick and was at the Oakland children's hospital. So I went to go visit him and prayed that he would get better. I told Gordy that my son was real sick and I had to be strong for him and I needed her love and support.

So Gordy went with me to Oakland to visit my son, then when we got back from our visit, we went to her mother's house. Gordy asked me if I wanted some loving after the long drive, so we went to the room and got to the lovemaking. It made all my pain just go away. My little Albert was only five years old when this had happened. It all looked very bad for him at this time; all I could do was pray to the Lord up above. It brought me and Gordy closer. Well, when we were done with our lovemaking, Gordy asked me if she could stay with me at my sister's house. "Hey, sure, if that's the way you feel." So she got her stuff and moved in with me. We were doing just fine, but without me working, money was not right. We would just make the best of it and watch some movies. My sister had a little girl about six months older than Destiny, so they would play together. We got our own room; Gordy still had some love for me, her baby's daddy. We would take our little sexy shower shots together. Boy oh boy, this made the rest of the day that much more beautiful. I was selling some oldie cassettes to make just a little bit of money. It worked; I would go to the stores and hit up the people who liked oldies and sold them, $5 for one and $20 for five. So we would have money for some movies and something to eat, plus gas. This was going pretty good, but I still had to turn myself in. So I asked my Gordy to give me some sweet loving, then I would go turn myself into jail. My sister took me to the main jail, and they shot me down and told me to wait till it turned into a warrant. So we went back to my sister's house and told Gordy what had took place. "What the heck, babe, it has to wait." So we were on hold. Gordy was already in bed and told me to tuck her in, so we made some more love.

Then after about a week went by, Gordy started wanting to get high again. She called her homeboy who had the stuff, and he took advantage of the situation and just gave it to her. That was what hurt the most; I had known the homeboy. Then I did not know if he was connected to the *familia*. For if he was, he was untouchable; you'd need permission to take flight. Plus I did not want any trouble in front of my precious Destiny or her mother. What was I gonna do?

I still had words with this so-called homeboy. I told him, "Gordy is my beloved northern Azteca queen, mother of my one and only daughter. She's not just another woman. She is very precious to me. So please show some respect, at least for my Destiny. With this understanding, whatever you feed the mother of my daughter is out of my hands. Hey, just don't put your hands on my Destiny or little Julian." Then I told him that whenever Gordy would call me, I'd be right here. Then we went for a little ride, like I was scared or something. I got Gordy saying that she didn't love me anymore and to leave her alone. So I bowed out gracefully and left her alone. Before I left, I did give Julian and Destiny a hug and kiss. I had to swallow up my pride and humble myself. *Let me be the bigger and better man and walk away.*

Then about a week later, I asked Julian if he wanted to go camping with me and my sister as family. I told Julian, "Just because your mother and I are not together doesn't mean that we can't still hang out." So he got his stuff and went camping with me. We got back to that Mother Nature and father time. Then we made our little trails and got situated. We got some snacks and ate and drank. We went for walks up the main paths, like true northern Aztec warriors. For now we walked the land, like our beloved forefathers. Then we took a small little break and started to talk warrior to warrior. Julian told me, "Thank you for bringing me with you camping. I just do not like that man who gets my mother high all the time, Chino."

"Yeah, I know just how you must feel, Julian. Hey, what can we do but just pray that your mother starts to see that there ain't no future in that, smoking that stuff? Love is a crazy thing sometimes. For it is better to love and lost than to never have loved at all."

Julian and I headed back to our campsite. We started making a little something for dinner on the hot plates. It was all good; we got full and started cleaning up. We started telling some stories about when my sister and I were young growing up then some of the trouble that we had got into as kids, hoping that there might be a lesson to be learned to the good. It was getting late, so we got ready to go to sleep. All that I could do was think about Destiny.

Well, we finally fell asleep; Julian was right next to me. We got up the next morning and washed up. Then we got some breakfast and went on some more trails. We got to this one bench. I carved *Chino and Gordy* into the corner of the bench; it came out clean. We started to walk some more, checking out all the beautiful things around us—the birds and the waterfalls. Then we hiked back to our campsite. We started to get a little hungry and cooked something to eat. Then we listened to some gangster oldies, enjoying these sad songs right before we got ready to fall asleep. Julian and I began to pray for my daughter and his mother. The next morning, we packed our stuff and went over to my sister's house. Then I got my wheels. "Hey, Julian, get your stuff and get ready so I can take you back to your mother." When we got to the house of Gordy's mother, Gordy was not looking too good. "Hey, girl, just bringing back your mijo safe and sound." Then I told Gordy, "You do not look so good." She looked very weak. Yeah, she had known this was true. "Where's everybody when you are down and out for the count?" So I helped her up and took her to the hospital. I had Destiny and Julian; we were waiting outside. I was playing with Julian and Destiny till they had finished with Gordy. We finally went back inside to see what the problem was with Gordy. All they said was that she needed to take better care of herself. I got ready to take her home, and Gordy wanted to stay with me once again. So I took advantage of the situation. I kind of kidnapped my baby's mother so she couldn't get high on that stuff anymore. I was saving her from herself. *That's my Azteca Queen. Let me bring her back to reality.* Gordy needed some good rest and good food; I would feed her in bed if she wanted. We did our little honeymoon thing for just a little while. I was not complaining; at least I could keep my Destiny close to me—and Julian. It was like the Lord told me to forgive the mother of my daughter. It was wishful thinking, I guess, on my part. Now Gordy might feel true love.

CHAPTER 10

JUST FINISHED DOING ONE HUNDRED DAYS AND NIGHTS LOCKED UP

I loved Gordy to the fullest and was just trying to show her how much. I was blind over her. Time just stood still whenever we were together. Well, after about two weeks, Gordy was looking a lot better and back to normal. She was looking so much more beautiful. We got our lovemaking late at night and took our shower shots about lunchtime. This was good for both of us; our daughter saw that we were happy. Then when Gordy was nice and healthy one more time, now she called her brother to come pick her up so she could move back to her mother's house. I just about cried on the inside. Just to see her leave for no reason was just breaking my heart. I had to deal with this the very best that I could at the time. Then about a week later, I got arrested in front of my sister's house. Now at least I could do this time and start over when I got back to work again.

When I got to jail and housed, I started to write some love letters to Gordy and little letters to Destiny. But in my heart, I knew that Gordy wouldn't respond or write me back. So I was doing my push-ups, trying to stay strong, reading, and talking to the other inmates. Then I was reading my Bible, thinking on a positive note. We were having some spreads, breaking bread with the rest of the homeboys. So my time was passing along pretty good. Seeing these men facing some hard time, like fifteen and twenty years in prison, hey, why was I feeling sad about my short time? I started going to some classes about relationships and anger management, trying to better myself for when I'm free once again. What had I learn about my own past relationships, like about me and Gordy? There was verbal abuse as well as putting hands on a woman. There was give-and-take, not only taking but giving as well—like doing some of the house chores together, not just letting the woman do all the work around the house. So now I was about thirty days to the house, and my time was going pretty fast. I was still sending out my love letters to Gordy, just getting my feelings hurt. I was still keeping the faith about Gordy.

Some of my friends tried to talk to me to up lift my spirits; that worked. "Hey, maybe she has moved on without you. Now it's time for you to move on yourself, and don't trip, bro. Let's go out into the sundeck and look at the other pretty *mamacitas* outside." So we went there, and this one looked up at us. Hey, I started to get at her, and she was a very pretty Azteca princess. "Thanks for making my day." I got her attention. "Hey, what's your name?" She said Linda. "Well, my name is William, but they call me Chino." Then I told her that I'd be busting out real soon. Then I told her that I would need some female company. "What do you say, Ms. Linda? It's a date."

She said, "You are crazy."

Then I told her to say my name.

"Why?"

"Just to hear you say it."

"Alright then. Chino."

I told her, "Thank you. Love you for that." Then she gave me her phone number. "I'll call you when I get out. Alrighty then, take care of your fine self."

My homeboy said, "How did you do that, Chino? Pull that female from way up here."

"It's all about the way that you speak to these females. They call it the gift of gab. Make them smile and never make them feel sad."

This way, I got a little something to look forward to when I'd bust out. Still, here I was sending Gordy another love letter, praying that I could get her back. I knew that the other men in my tank were saying, "Chino won't get a letter from his Gordy." I was feeling like a fool, but it was cool. Then all of a sudden, like a small miracle, I did get a letter from Gordy. Man oh man, with her lipstick traces all over it, it was very sexy. Then she sent me a photo of my Destiny. Now there was a little bit of hope that we would be together once again. Hey, that made my day, and now I knew that she was in Arizona; that was good by me. What was funny about this letter was that I was thinking about that song, "I Destroyed Your Love for Me." I had written in my love letter the very same song. Hey, it was not how far we were but how close we stayed. So this made me feel great. I was showing these friends of mine. "Check this out."

They said, "That's faraway gangster love, brother. Now stay strong."

So then I said, "I do love you, Gordy. Shaw, baby doll. I got crazy love for my Destiny." Thank you, Lord, for all my blessings, and forgive me for all my sins.

Well, in about a week, they said, "Ruiz, roll up your gear for release."

"All right, my brothers, may our Lord bless you. Stay strong and keep your heads up. For I do, San Jo, love you." I was gone like the wind that brought me in this place. I was not a bad boy—just a boy who had it bad. Oh, what a feeling when you did get out. Man oh man. Then I caught the bus to my dad's house. My sister had moved out of San Jo, so my dad told me that I could stay with him. He had my Monte Carlo waiting for me. It was cool for him to do that. My dad had a trailer home right on Monterey Road. "Hey, Pops, I just got out. Let me get situated."

"Yeah, mijo, it's all good."

It was October 1997. Then we went to dinner and caught up. Then on Monday, I went to my old job to see if I could start working again. I was a machine operator; I had known how to run all the machines. They told me that I could start working on swing shift. "No problem. I'll be here and ready to work."

"Alrighty then, we'll see you on Monday afternoon at 3:30 p.m."

"Cool." I got back home and told my dad the good news.

"Hey, that's the spirit."

So we went to get some breakfast across the street. My job was about three miles away. Well, I drove my Monte to work and back home. Then this one day, before work, I was getting some lunch for work. I saw this cop car parked in the parking lot. Soon as my order was ready, I got into my Monte and started to leave to my job. I looked into my mirror and saw this cop right behind me, and he pulled me over. So I pulled over and then got out of the car; he took me to the side and gave me a break. I showed him my paperwork. I was driving on a revoked driver's license. Then he gave me back my paperwork and told me that he was going to tow my Monte but was not going to put a thirty-day hold on it; that was cool. In my paperwork, there was a joint, and he did not see it, so I smoked it right after the cop had left and my car was towed.

So I walked to work and told my boss what had happened; he gave me the day off. He told me, "Don't trip. Just go get your Monte back." Then I caught the bus home and told my dad. Well, the next day, we caught the bus to the police department and got a release form, which cost about $100. Then we went to the tow yard and paid another $300 to bail my Monte out. Altogether, it cost me about $500. I got the car back to my dad's trailer and parked it there. I learned my lesson. I found a bike that cost fifty bucks and started to ride it to work and back home. That was not so bad. It was a straight down Monterey then you'd turn on San Jose Avenue. I would stop and get my lunch and take it with me to the job. Then Gordy had sent me her phone number in Arizona. So we got to talk long-distance, then I could talk to my Destiny. Then this was right before Thanksgiving, so I asked Gordy if I could go and visit her and Destiny and Julian. So she said, "That would be fine, but don't think that we are back together." She said that she had lived with her grandmother, so we should show respect. That was cool with me; I just wanted to see Gordy. So we were talking more and more on the phone. Then I started saving up some money for my trip. This was too good to be true; I was finally going to see my Azteca princess with her blessing. I could feel that even Gordy was starting to flirt with me over the phone. She told me that she missed me tucking her into bed and that she was nice and healthy and got her sexy bedroom body back. "Hey, Gordy, you just don't know how much I miss all of you guys." It was funny from so far away how happy Gordy made me feel. So then I told some of the guys at work that I was leaving to Arizona to get my visit on with my Gordy and my daughter.

"Hey, that sounds cool, bro. You just be careful out there."

"Yeah." Then I told my dad about me going over to Arizona to visit my daughter and her mother.

He told me the same thing. "You just be careful out there. Don't get yourself caught up."

"Hey, let me get back to my baby."

So then I decided to get me a camera to take some photos on my visit, then I could have some good memories. I started to get my stuff ready for my trip, then I would be good to go. Yeah, I got the green light from my love, Gordy. It was good to know that I would be welcomed with open arms when I got up there. Everything was perfect in my little world. I was just about walking on air. Now I could dwell on happiness—that there was no tension between me and Gordy. I'd watch my every step to not be saying the wrong thing about other men. I was just thinking about how nice it would finally be to have Gordy back in my arms again. So as we were still talking on the phone, Gordy was telling me that her butt got bigger—in a good way—and that her breasts got bigger too. Man, I could not wait to see for myself. I told her, "Is that right? You are looking sweet, and I'm gonna eat you up when I get over there." She laughed, then she let me talk to Destiny and Julian. I told Destiny that her daddy would be there pretty soon and couldn't wait to see her. Now I was motivated and dedicated, and I missed her too much. Gordy understood that I was still staying healthy, doing my gangster workout, and doing my push-ups. Hey, don't all females really feel sexy when you're making love to them and you are sexy in your own way? It goes both ways. Men and women like that animal attraction, in the best way.

Finally, the night came. Right after work, I went to the Greyhound bus station with all my stuff for my long trip. I got my suitcase and bought my ticket to Arizona. I got my little Walkman, listening to some music to help me on this long bus ride. Now we stopped at all the little towns along the way, then we stopped to get something to eat. My round-trip ticket cost me about one hundred and twenty bucks. *Giddyap, let's start to get ghost and leave my hometown.* All good things do come to those who wait. We could not get to Arizona fast enough. Now we were rolling. *Just keep the pedal to the metal, Mr. Bus Driver.* Finally, we got to Los Angeles and got put on another bus. Talk about getting sick of fast food—well, I was. I really did not mind the stop in LA; we could get off the bus and get to stretch our body from this long bus ride. Then we could get our smoke on outside. Then we got back on the bus for another eight hours.

Finally, we got to Arizona; as soon as I got there, I called up Gordy and told her that I was at the bus station. "Hey, babe, come and pick me up." She said that she was on her way. Then in about ten minutes, she got there. When we saw each other, she gave me a nice, long kiss, and I got my stuff and put it in the car. She came with her tia. So we went to the house of Gordy's grandma; we began to chill out there and started to drink some beers. I put my stuff away in the room. Well, we were drinking in the backyard, then Gordy made me a plate of Thanksgiving dinner. That hit the spot, that's for sure. Then I went back outside and opened another brew. Gordy had her girl cousin there, and she asked to sit on my lap. I said, "No, I got Gordy." This got Gordy mad; there was a little tension now between them. Then her family hit me up and asked if I was a Norteño; I said that I represented my hometown in a good way. They asked to see the tattoo on my stomach, so I showed them with a tight six-pack abs that I was doing my workout. It was no secret about me feeding the sharks. Booyah, I was nice and healthy. I didn't sing it; I brought it. I wasn't new to this; I was true to this representing my hometown, San Jo, Northern California. Hey, the females loved this stuff, like being down for your hometown. So we kept getting our drink on, and the girls were feeling a little buzzed. So was I just a little bit. Then we went back inside the house, and Gordy and her cousin started a little cat fight. We let them go at it for a minute, then we broke them up. It was starting to get late, and I went to Gordy's bedroom and got ready for bed. Then Gordy followed me in. She was still feeling sexy and told me, "How dare my cousin try to sit on your lap." So we were both in the room. I locked the door and got into my boxers, yes.

So now we were finally all alone, making up for lost time. Then we started to kiss and make out. Things were finally getting hot and heavy. Gordy got in her sexy little panties, and we started to make love. It had been so long, I busted one right away. Then we stopped and went at it again in a little while. Man oh man, this was what I had been waiting for, like going to heaven once again. She had missed my making love to her; she showed me that. What a blessing it was to have her back in my arms, Gordy filling me with her sexy charms. Then we finally went to sleep with a smile on our face. Well, we got up the next morning, and I got to see Destiny and Julian. They gave lots of hugs and kisses to me, and I gave them back. Then I met Gordy's grandma. "She tells me you are Destiny's father."

"Yes, that would be me. I came all the way from San Jose to visit them. Thank you for letting me into your home." Then I knelt down on one knee and gave her a kiss on her hand to show my utmost respect. Then I played with Destiny and Julian outside; they were riding bikes. So I thanked the Lord for all his blessings and for getting me there nice and safe. Then Gordy started cooking us some breakfast, good old home cooking—tortillas with bacon and *papas*. Oh my goodness, Gordy told me that she couldn't believe that I came all the way from San Jo to visit her and Julian and Destiny. "Look how happy Destiny and Julian are to see you, Chino. As I am too— as you knew from last night when I showed you and we made love almost all night long."

Then Gordy's tia Blanca came to visit her. "Hey, Gordy, want to come to my house with Chino and chill out there?"

They asked me. "That sounds cool with me." So we got our stuff and got Julian and Destiny, and we drove to her house and picked up some more brew. All was just perfect in my world, even just for a little while. Then they got drive-through liquor stores in Phoenix, Arizona; that was a trip. Then I went to the window and got some snacks and a six-pack and a twelve-pack of Coronas.

We finally got to Blanca's house—it was in the next town, Scottsdale—and started to get situated. We got our stuff out of the car. Then we went inside and started to get our little drink on. Then we started to listen to some gangster oldies. Blanca and I hit it off right from the gate. She liked the way that I came all the way from Northern California just to visit. She also liked the 49ers, as I did. She had a daughter who was just as old as Destiny, so they got to play together. So we all were having a good time and called for a pizza and ate our dinner. This time was passing by not too fast, but I knew that it wouldn't last forever. It only hurt when it was time to get back to San Jo. Oh well, I would not miss seeing Gordy and Destiny and Julian even just for a couple of days and nights. I was living my dream, and it was all good. I was in heaven right here on Mother Earth. If anyone knew what this was worth, it was priceless. Could you put a price on true love? Blessings from our Lord up above. Well, at Blanca's house, we got our own room, and it was that magic time for bed. We got into the bedroom, and Destiny was already asleep. So now Gordy and I started to make good love, and it felt so good to both of us. She let me take some sexy photos of her looking all sexy—something to hold me till I could come back to visit. The next morning, we made love in the shower, and that was beautiful—what a way to start a Sunday. Gordy knew that later on tonight, I would have to get back to the bus station and leave back. The day went by so fast; now I was getting my stuff ready. Gordy and I made love one more time before I went. She started to cry, and I cried on the inside. Then I wiped away her tears; we cried together. "Let's keep our heads up, and give me a smile, my lover." We pulled ourselves together and made the best of it. We told and showed our love for each other. I was ready to leave and got all my stuff in the car, and we all went to the bus station. Gordy took me and greeted me off and told me, "Thank you for coming to visit. I love you."

Gordy had given long love when we were together; we had just made up for all the lost time. Then she gave me all kinds of love bites. She gave me kisses as sweet as wine, kisses as sweet as candy, soothing to my taste. I asked Gordy if it was fine with her for me to come back at Christmas. She said that would be just fine. I would be counting the days and the nights. I said, "There ain't no mountain high enough to keep me from getting to you, baby. For there ain't no stopping us now. So you stay strong till I get back to you, my darling baby. Now give me a precious kiss to seal the deal." Now I got my stuff and put it on the bus and got ready to leave. I waved and blew her a kiss; she did the same with tears in her eyes. I guess it was all in the crazy game of love. What a long bus ride back, but I was still riding high on Gordy's love. Then what a beautiful, good visit. I did thank my Gordy for sharing her precious body with me. It still put a tingle in my spine; she was mine oh mine. Then putting a smile on Destiny's pretty face was priceless—and Julian's too. Getting to touch my precious daughter just for a little while was all good by me.

Finally, I got back to home base, San Jo. Then I went to my dad's house and checked in. I told my dad how good my long trip was. When Monday came, I was ready to go back to work. "Hey, what's up, fellas?"

"So how was the trip to see your daughter?"

"All that I can say is that it went beautifully."

They said, "We can tell. Look at you, Chino, with all those love bites."

"What can I say? Why, I ain't got nothing to be ashamed about. I got there and got to handle my business in the bedroom. Gordy missed her baby's daddy. Hey, check this out. They got drive-through liquor stores."

"Man, that's crazy—loco."

"But it's true." Then I told them, "I took some photos of the precious Gordy and my kids that you guys might get a kick of. Now let's go get this money, baby boy." The next day, I took the photos and took them to work, not the sexy ones.

"Man, your daughter looks so pretty, and she's getting so big. Look at her always smiling. Pretty."

I was the king of my surroundings when I was up there in Arizona. Even the president of the company would ask me, "How's your Azteca princess and our Glassforms baby?"

Then I would tell him, "She is fine. Here, take a look at these photos."

"Nice. All right, let's get back to work." Then he'd tell me to keep up the good work.

So we got our lunch about 8:00 p.m. We'd eat and talk then smoke a cigarette before we went back to our machines. Then I was showing off my precious photos of Gordy and Destiny. Hey, don't all children love to take photos of them? "Smile for me, baby." Then Gordy always liked to give her sexy smile. Destiny was such a pretty little girl, and a photo said it all. So I asked Gordy on the phone again if it would be all right with her for me to go back for Christmas.

"Yeah, it's all good."

I was just checking, staying within my boundaries, and not taking her for granted. I didn't want her to feel any pressure from me, for anything might happen from so far away.

My foreman lived right next door to the family that killed my little brother—what a small world. He also had a daughter about the same age as my Destiny. We would take our lunch and talk about what was going on in our surroundings and our San Jo city of no pity for the weak of heart. We would read the paper and listen to some music. Then I was back to the machine that I ran, for sometimes, the machine could run you to the ground. That was if you let it and let it get the best of you. I was a machine operator 2, status. So every check, I would put a little money away for my trip back to Arizona. Then it was going to be Christmas. I had someone rebuilding my car engine for the Monte Carlo, so I rode my bike back and forth to work, good exercise at the same time. Sometimes on the way back home from work, I would get pulled over for no reason. Those cops were always messing with me. I got used to it after a while; I got nothing to hide but my pride as an Aztec warrior, and that was no crime. The cops were questioning me, like what was my name. Then the cops asked me where I was coming from. I told them I was getting off work, so they let me go. This would happen about two times a week for about a month. Then I would get home from work about 12:30 a.m.

When I got to my dad's trailer, I would chill out, relax, write a love letter to Gordy, and send in a few lines for Destiny. Then I'd get some sleep, get up about ten thirty in the morning, wash up, eat, watch some TV till twelve, start to do my workout till about one thirty, wash up, then take a shower. I would call my Gordy about four times a week long-distance, so I would not want to make a big phone bill so we could stay in touch as much as I could. It would make my day right before I had to work to hear Gordy's and Destiny's voice. "Hi, Daddy, when are you coming to see me? I miss you, my daddy, and I love you, Daddy."

"First, your daddy has to go to work and make this money so I can get you some presents for you and your brother, Julian, at Christmas." Then I would tell Julian and Destiny that they had to listen to their mother, Gordy, always. "You be a good little angel for your daddy, and let me talk to your brother. Hey, what's up, mijo? How are you doing? I miss you, little man of the house." Then Julian and I finished our little talk.

"Let me get my mother so you guys can talk."

"Hey, my Azteca princess, how's everything going out there?"

"Your daughter is trouble, just like her daddy."

Then I told her, "You knew it was trouble when you walked into this job. Just joking, my love. Can't wait to see you again. Now it's only about two more weeks till we can get together."

Gordy started to tease me over the phone. "What are you gonna do to me when you come back over here?"

"You tell me. What do want me to do to you, Gordy?"

"Oh, I don't really know."

"You will find out when I get back to where you are. I'm gonna spank that pretty ass of yours then kiss you all over your precious bedroom body and give you love bites." So we got our little sweet talk on. Then before we got off the phone, I said, "Blow me a kiss."

"You have to wait, my lover."

"Babe, that sounds good to me, and ain't no thing like the real thing, *que no?*" Then I got myself ready to get to work. I was ready for my long bike ride. I pulled over at this one hot links spot and got me something before I got to work. I ate half then saved the rest for my lunch. Then we had across the street from work this sandwich deli. Sometimes I would get me a hot sandwich at lunchtime then eat it back at work. I always tried to have a good meal after working so hard. See, at my dad's trailer, the stove was not working, so I had to go get me something to grub on. I did not mind one bit. Well, I would also check and see how my engine was coming along. I would pay this garage about $100 a week till it was done; it cost me $1,600. That was not bad at all back in 1998, 'member, you member. Well, this being written, I believe this to be true. My Monte would be out of the shop real soon. Then I was going to my driving classes to get my driver's license back. I had to go to six months of classes; that was no problem. I knew that it would be greater later. Then I would be good to go, driving my Monte with a rebuilt engine; it still had a good paint job. Hey, if you knew San Jo, you'd know that on Monterey Road, you got access to everything—bus stop and all this eats right up and down the street.

One day, I was just about finished doing my workout right outside of my dad's trailer. Then the manager's son was checking out the lot and hit me up, "You Bill's son?"

"Yes."

Then he was checking out that everybody was keeping their space nice and clean. We started to talk, and he asked me if I was a Norteño. "Why, no, I represent San Jo to the fullest." We got along. He had a clean BMW with a cool sound system. "You are big pimping, John."

Then he told me, "Your dad don't look like he would have a Norteño son."

"Well, that just goes to show you that you just can't judge everyone from the way they look. No disrespect, but I need to do some more sets of push-ups. Handle your business then, brother."

So I was finished doing my sets of push-ups. Then we started talking—John and I. We were checking out this female out the corner of our eye. "Hey, she looks kinda cool."

I said that she looked all right. Then I asked John, "Would you hit that, carnal?"

He said, "For sure. Look at her shaking it for us, trying to be sexy as can be."

So I told him that she was no Jennifer Lopez. Then I asked John, "Let me get at you for a minute. Your mother seems to be all over my dad around here. Do you think that you could ask her to back off just a little bit? Do me this favor, and I'll see what I can do for you."

"Hey, William, you got a lot of ink on you. I can't believe that your dad is a White man."

"Check this out. He is German and Italian. He is my true father. It's that my mother is an Azteca princess."

Then John said, "You are up on your bloodline."

"Yeah, I do my homework." I said that I was old-school and new-school all in one package. So then John told me that he would speak to his mother about not sweating my dad anymore; that sounded cool. That was the end of our little talk. "Hey, thanks for hearing me out, and have a good one, John."

"You do the same, Chino."

Then I went back inside and washed up. I was trying to relax before I had to go to work. On my way to work, I stopped and got a rice bowl for my lunch. I finally made it to work and looked at the local news and saw that this one guy was killed by the cops. Well, this guy was the little brother of the man who killed my little brother. What a trip; what goes around comes back around. Then I showed the paper to my friend Sly, my foreman. "Look at who got killed." I felt that it was a small payback for what had happened to my little brother in a funny way. Then I said a small prayer for my little brother; after all these years, now that family would know the feeling of putting someone they loved deep in the ground. That's not a good feeling for anybody. Hey, I guess that's the way of the world. Well, may he rest in peace, anyways. I had left it in God's hands now; I washed my hands of what had happened.

I would not tell a lie. When I had got off work and got home, I thanked our Lord and wished that they would feel my pain to the fullest. I had forgiven, but I had not forgotten my little bro. "So please forgive me, Lord, if this was a sin." I felt like this was a blessing for our family. Everybody pays sooner or later.

So it was about one more week till Christmas; yes, I was just counting down the days and nights. This time went by really fast; I just stayed busy at work. Then I went to get some little presents for Gordy, Destiny, and Julian. Then I had got Gordy a pretty ring with a red garnet. It cost me about $300; I was making payments. Then I got Destiny a Tickle Me Elmo, then I'd take Julian to the store and he could pick out his own gift. Well, the day was finally here, and I got everything ready for my trip back to Arizona. I told all the homeboys at work that I would be going back to visit my baby's mother. They told me to have a good time over there and to take care of myself. They gave me gangster love. "I will see you gangsters when I get back to work." My dad gave me a ride to the bus station and sent me off. I got my round-trip ticket, put my stuff on the bus, and got going on this long ride. This bus driver could not drive fast enough; we finally got to LA to get on the next bus. Yes, we were halfway there; only halfway to go, then I would be back in my baby's arms. So we finally got there, and I called Gordy. "Hey, babe, come and get me." Then she got there in about ten minutes. I got all my stuff ready when she picked me up. When Gordy picked me up, we started to kiss and hug. I put my stuff into the car, and we went back to her grandmother's house. Then I got my stuff out the car and put them inside Gordy's bedroom. That was a good feeling—right here at last. That all the hard work was finally paying off. Then I changed into my sweats and started to relax, and we had some Coronas, chilling outside in the backyard. We were enjoying the night air, watching the kids playing. Then I gave Destiny her little Tickle Me Elmo.

So while we were in the backyard, I got my camera and started taking some photos of Julian and Destiny for my memories. Then it started to get late, and the kids went inside and got ready for bed. They slept in the living room. I gave them a hug and a kiss. Then we finished drinking, and Gordy and I did the same. I could not wait to make sweet love to Gordy, and she felt the same way. She put on a sexy teddy bear outfit, so I took some photos of her looking all sexy for me. Then we got out little freak on; whoa, to be making mad love to her was like my dream come true. When we woke up, I got some more of that sweet love from Gordy. She was lying close to me early in the morning; I could not help it. Then my Destiny woke me up and gave me a good morning kiss. "Daddy, wake up and watch cartoons with me." Then she wanted to play with her Tickle Me Elmo. Then I took some more photos of Destiny; she looked so pretty.

Destiny always gave some nice big smiles. Then I let my Gordy get some more sleep; when she woke up, we had begun to make some breakfast. We all got to eat, and then we cleaned up. So then Julian and I went outside to play. Destiny was showing me that she could ride her brand-new bike. "Hey, that's it, mija. You are doing good."

Then Julian started to show me his skills on his bike. "Hey, Chino, watch me jump over the little ramp."

"Cool, mijo. You did good, like a pro."

Then we went back inside the house; it was really hot outside. Gordy just wanted to kick back and watch a movie with me. After we were done with one movie, the kids and I walked to the store for some chips and ice cream, then I got a six-pack of Coronas for me and Gordy. Then we started to get our drink on. Gordy's brother started telling this story that I had left him when he was surrounded by all kinds of scraps, like I was scared or something; well, that was not the true story. Then I asked her brother to fill me in. He was trying to make me feel like a sidebuster or a punk; that was not true on mine. I told him, "Be nice already, brother." So her brother, Chango, and I let it rest. We gave each other a gangster hug. Then we all had a good time regardless. He knew that he was lying all along; now everybody else knew this too. I got a gangster reputation to uphold as a northern Aztec warrior. I'd never step back and stay ready to attack the enemy. I let that go and just let that roll off my back. For now, let me get back and focus on my Gordy, Julian, and Destiny. Nothing was going to mess up my good time with my little family. After coming all the way over here, I had to make the best of it—keeping a smile on Gordy's and Destiny's face. "Come here, Destiny, and sit by Daddy and Mama. Let me take a photo of you looking so beautiful, my little Azteca princess. Your daddy loves you too much. How old are you now, mija?"

"I'm four."

"I know you are getting so big already, my baby girl."

Gordy started to get mad. "Hey, what about me, daddy?"

"Hey, baby doll, you look just as pretty. Destiny takes after you. She is blessed with all your beauty. Thank you for letting me be the father of your first mija."

We were still getting along just fine, drinking some Coronas and watching some movies. Then we started smooching on the sofa, like we were on our honeymoon or something. Now it was Christmas Eve, and we started to open all our presents. Everybody was happy. Gordy started to open up my present and put on the ring, and it fit her perfectly. We took a photo and started to take some more photos of all the kids opening their little presents. Gordy got me some lowrider shirts. Hey, Gordy was my special present, and I couldn't wait to unwrap her later. I also got Gordy some gangster oldie CDs so she would have something to listen to. Now all the kids were ready for bed, and it had been a long day and night. So Gordy and I went to the bedroom, and she put on a sexy little teddy bear outfit, and she looked so sexy. I asked for some more photos, and she said yes. She started posing for me, looking as sexy as could be. Then she came to bed, and we made some great love. I busted one then one more. It seemed that our sex was blessed from heaven up above; all this precious love was just for us both.

Then when I had got up with Gordy all naked and warm, I had to get some more of her, waking up with that morning woody; she did the trick. Gordy's body was thick; she had sexy, silky thighs and a heart-shaped butt and those nice breasts—whoa, like my own Playboy Bunny. The angels must have been singing when we made love. So I should enjoy all this precious loving as long as I could. Then we got up and took that shower shot. After this, we got ready for our breakfast and ate. I helped Gordy clean up the mess in house. It was already getting hot. Then we watched the kids play with all their gifts. Then Gordy's tia Blanca came over and asked us to chill out at her house for the night. Hey, that sounded cool, so we went. We got our little stuff ready for the night; Gordy showed Blanca the ring that I had got for her. Then I started to play some of the gangster oldies that I had got for Gordy. We needed to drive to the next town and stop at the store for some brew and some snacks. We got to Blanca's house; she had a two-story home—much bigger than Gordy's grandma's. So I knew that Blanca liked the 49ers and a got her a jersey for Christmas. Then she put it on the wall in her living room. So we took a couple of photos of her with Gordy. When we had finished, we ordered a pizza, so we did not have to cook. It was so hot already. Blanca took some photos of me and Gordy hugging and kissing. We were all smiling, having a ball; that was priceless to me and Gordy. Then Gordy had put all kinds of love bites on me, and I had put some on Gordy too. Yeah, I was on top of the world, and it was all good. Even if it was just for a little while, I should enjoy this till it'd end. They were drinking some Bud Lights; I was drinking my Coronas but not getting drunk, just mellow. Now it started to get late, and the kids were getting ready for bed. Gordy and I were feeling a little sexy, and we got ready for bed ourselves. We got busy between the sexy sheets and made tender sweet love.

So we started fooling around. Gordy asked if I wanted to take some more photos of her being all sexy—just a little something to hold me from so far away. Then I got my camera, and Gordy started to give me some sexy poses. I tell her, "Let me see you smile, then let me see those pretty breasts." Gordy was a natural, like my own model. I took about five sexy shots of her looking like a beauty. I told her, "You are my love goddess, and thank you for sharing your precious bedroom body with me." Then I got to unwrap her.

She told me, "Have me, Chino. Make love to me before you get ready to leave. I'm yours as you are all mine. Now let's become one under the moon and the sun." She said that our love was built on a healthy foundation of true love. Then we had that understanding and trust.

Well, my time was just about up, and I must be getting back to San Jo—sad but true. We started feeling just a little sad—both of us. I could see that Gordy was starting to cry, so we cried together. Then I wiped away her tears, and she wiped mine. "Alrighty then, my Aztec princess. Baby, don't you cry. Jove is here standing bye. I don't wanna see no more tears coming out my baby doll's eyes. Now let's pick ourselves, back up, and turn this frown upside down. Smile for me already." We gave each other some hugs and kisses. "So let me get my things together, my love. Hey, Destiny and Julian, I'm getting ready to go back. Let me get some hugs and kisses before I leave."

Destiny told me, "Daddy, I love you, and call me when you get back home."

Then I put my stuff in the car and got ready to go to the bus station. Gordy was still crying just a little bit and gave me some more hugs and lovely kisses, sweet as candy. I wished that I did not have to leave. Hey, it was out of my hands; I still had my job waiting for me. So now I was just waiting for my bus to get ready to leave. When I heard the bus getting ready to get back to San Jo, I gave Gordy one last kiss then got my stuff and got on the bus. Now I got situated for my long bus ride back.

What a blessing it was to be with Gordy and Destiny even just for a week, and we got to spend New Year's together. Now I was on my way back to San Jo, and I was still high on Gordy's sweet love. So I said a little silent prayer. "Thank you, Lord, for looking down on me and my family." Finally, I was back to home base, and I got off the bus and got my stuff. Then I got back to my dad's trailer and got myself situated. I started to talk to my dad and told him what a great time I had.

So then my dad said, "I can tell you had a good time. Look at your neck all bit up. That Gordy must be a real tiger."

Yes, she was. "Hey, you want to go and get some breakfast across the street?" I was still walking on air from still being fresh and from coming back from seeing Gordy, Julian, and Destiny. "Hey, Dad, I sometimes feel like you with my three kids, two boys, and one daughter." Then our food was ready, and we started to eat while the food was still hot. We finished our breakfast.

My dad asked, "So how's little Destiny?"

"She is getting big and so pretty just like her mother."

"Hey, that's good. I say that Gordy has you on cloud nine."

So then I got ready to take my shower, and I saw Gordy had given me all kinds of love bites on my stomach—real sexy, like she missed San Jo to the fullest. I started getting ready to get back to work, then I had got my photos back from my trip. I had to make sure that I took all the real-sexy photos of Gordy out for myself—my private stash. But I still had some of Destiny and me and Gordy still looking sexy. I was grateful to have my fun in the Arizona sun. Finally, I got to work. "Hey, what's up, my gangster homeboys? And Happy New Year."

Then they said, "What's the matter with you, Chino?"

"Just got back From Arizona, and I'm walking on air. Ain't nobody going to mess up my good feeling." I showed them some photos and let them be the judge.

They all came back smiling from ear to ear. "Now we know why you are so happy, bro. She looks like a Playboy Bunny, and that little daughter looks so pretty."

Then I saw my supervisor. "Check out my Destiny, brother."

So my supervisor and I saw each other at lunchtime. "Hey, your daughter looks happy." Then he said, "I know why you are so happy, with all them love bites all over your neck. That mother of your daughter looks like an Azteca star—no disrespect."

We started to eat our lunch and listened to some oldies then smoked. "Hey, it's time to get back to work. My Destiny is what love has joined together, and that's a fact. Hey, Sly, how's your precious daughter?"

"She is getting big, like your daughter."

"Hey, we make our children with the seed of that precious love, *que no?*"

"Well, I never thought of it that way."

"That's the way I think of it. Just keeping it for real."

See, Sly and I grew up in the rough part of the eastside, and we had done our time in prison, but now we had worked hard for our little money—like some true northern Aztec warriors of the past. Now we lived in peace, not war anymore. Then sometimes after work, Sly would give me a ride back to my dad's trailer; that was cool.

One night after work, I was walking my bike in the trailer and saw that female whom we were checking out. "Hey, what are you doing out here so late at night, and where's your boyfriend?" She told me that he had got busted. "Oh, that's too bad." Then I asked her if she needed some company; she was smoking a cigarette. Then I told her, "Let me put my bike away, and I will come back out." Her name was Linda, and she wanted to smoke a joint, if I had one. "Sure, let me go inside, and let us get our smoke on. Be right back. Be silent. My stepmother might wake up." She waited for me to get back out, then she took off her sweatshirt, and all I could see were breasts right in front of me—real sexy. So we smoked that joint and started to make out. Then she told that she had been checking me out for a while. "Is that right?" Then I told her that I was checking her out too. We were still making out, then she asked me if I had any condoms. "Yes, let me go back inside and get one." She was good to go. Then

Linda said to me that she had fire between her legs. So I told her, "Let me put out that little hot fire, mama. Yeah, Linda, let me service that hot fire that you got, baby girl. You want some of that gangster love?"

She said, "For sure." So she pulled down her tight pants and then peeled off her moist little panties. Then she let me inside that hot little kitty cat—meow, meow—then she began to purr. Then I hit that till I busted one. Oh, what a feeling. I was hitting it from behind then started to pull her hair so softly. "Who's your daddy now? Say my name—Chino." We were under those lovely stars, and then we were done. She wiped herself and pulled up her little panties then her pants. Hey, I thanked her. "Good looking out, baby doll." Booyah. I wasn't one to spread lies, but listen to this, talk about trailer trash—hey, I was only kidding. She would make a good old lady, but not mine. That was a good one-nighter or something. Then we talked some more, and she asked about my gangster Monte Carlo. I told her that it was in the shop, getting the engine rebuilt. Then we said good night, and she went back to her trailer. It was all good by me; we said our little "Hi" and "What's up?" Her boyfriend got out in about a week. Hey, he knew her better than I did.

So I was still waiting for the Monte to get finished, and they were almost done with her. All right, little by little, she was coming together, for sure. Like I said, the paint was still decent, and I had a pretty good stereo system, ten-inch speakers, and a good amplifier. Then it was time for me to get back to visit my two angels in Arizona. Well, Gordy's mom had asked me when I was going back; I said in about a month. So in about a month, she hit me up, and I told her that I was good to go. Then she told me that her son had rented a van and that if I would drive all the way to Arizona, that would be cool. So we were on our way, and her son was driving in front of us in a black Mustang. I was following him till I had lost him on the freeway. We were lost in Pasadena, then it was all bad. Case in point was this ugly mess that was happening to me; we ended up getting pulled over trying to find the way back.

CHAPTER 11

GETTING CAUGHT UP IN LA JAILHOUSE

I told Gordy's mom, "Don't trip." Then I spoke to the officer, "What's the problem?" He said that I did not put my blinker on. "Hey, no biggie." Then he asked me for my driver's license. I noticed that Gordy's mom got real nervous—like she knew something that I did not. Well, the officer started asking me for the paperwork on the van. I did not know where it was at. I thought that I was just going to get a big, fat ticket; my driver's license was suspended. Then he wrote me out the ticket, and I signed it, and I thought that we would be all in the clear.

Then he told me that something still did not match. "I can't let you go just yet." Then he took us both out of the van and called for more police cars. Now I wondered what was really going on. "Wait right here and get your stuff out of the van." I had my gym bag with some clothes and my oldies tapes, then I had some money in my wallet; I gave it to Gordy's mom. Well then, I asked Gordy's mom where she was going from here, back to Arizona or back to San Jose; she was crying now. Then they put the handcuffs on me and took me to the Los Angeles Twin Towers Jail. Once we got there, they started to question me. "Now how did you get that van?" I told them that I thought that it was all legit and that it was rented by her son, who gave me the keys. So then they asked me where I was from, and I told them I was from Northern California, San Jose. Then they took me out of my shirt and looked at my tattoos. I had *San Jo* on my stomach and *Ruiz* on my back. Then they came back and told me that the van was stolen. My heart hit the floor, and it was all bad for me. Then on my dear paperwork, they put that I was a northern gang member, NF. I was just about crying on the inside. I wanted these officers to know that I was a marked man in this jailhouse and that it was no secret. They gave me my charges, and I kept telling them that I was from up north and asked if they'd ever heard of the San Jose Sharks, the hockey team. They thought that I was just going crazy or something. Then after this was all said and done, they put me in a cell.

Now I knew the score; I just got blindsided all at once. It's cool when you get caught up for something that you know you did wrong. *Pero* not when you are not aware of it. I put that on everything thing that I loved; I really thought that the van was rented. Here I was just trying to do something right, like visiting my one and only daughter. Then I wanted to see all four generations of my daughter all together at the same place and time. Then it was all blackness right before my eyes. Hey, everything happens for a reason, then all backfires. It felt like a was in a very bad dream or something. I had already known that the southern Latinos got no love for northern Latinos; there had been too much bloodshed. So I had known it was all bad for me. Then in my holding cell, there was a phone, so I got to call my people. It was Friday night when we left San Jose; I had been driving all night. Now it was Saturday morning when I had got pulled over and got busted. First, I called Gordy in Arizona and told her that I was in the LA jail and to keep me strong, and I talked to Destiny, my daughter. She told me that she would pray for me. I was still all mixed up. I was just trying not to go crazy. I started to pray in silent in my little corner. Just before, all was just perfect in my world. I was on my way to visit my family, and I had the oldies on, just driving and not making any trouble. I could not wait to get to Arizona and see Gordy. My precious lover, Gordy, asked me what the heck happened; I told her that we had got pulled over and they said that the van was stolen. The cops gave me a $30,000 bail, so I knew that I would not be getting out soon. I felt a lot better after talking to Gordy; it made me feel stronger. In my time of weakness, I was looking for something good to up lift my spirits. Then some other inmates were coming into the cell and did not ask me where I was from. That was a blessing for me; at the time, they were just thinking about their own charges, thank God. I'd never felt so all alone in all my life.

I knew that my life was in danger and that I was the enemy—according to the game between the southern Latinos and me being a northern Latino. It seemed that these cops had wanted me to get the shit kicked out of me or something. There was a war going on, and it had been going on for many years. First, it was only behind the prison walls, then it was on the streets. I had tried to make the cops understand that I was from the other side. I knew that these cops did not care anything about me or what might happen to me. Maybe they thought that I was just trying to be a northern Aztec warrior badass. They never offered me protective custody, so I never bothered to ask for some. So I was in the cell trying to make the best of it, and they brought us our lunch, some fried bean burritos—that was breakfast, lunch, and dinner. Then the next day, they moved me down to another cell just a couple of cells up. I could still watch some television. Then I started looking at all the different gangs on the wall with some of their nicknames. Then I still had my street clothes, my cutoffs and my shirt, plus my Nike's. Only the Lord and I knew that I was telling the truth and not guilty of this crime. Then I got in line for the phone and got my turn, and I called Gordy once again. I told Gordy to pray for me and to put Destiny back on the phone, and we talked. It was a blessing to hear her voice. I told her that her daddy loved her, then Destiny asked me, "What happened to you, Daddy?"

"Don't worry, mija. Just say a prayer that your daddy will stay strong." And we prayed together again. I was thinking of the book of Daniel—when he got thrown to prison, danced in the fire, and did not get burned, then they set him free. Then on my paperwork, right on the bottom, they put northern gang member, so I had to keep this undercover from the other inmates. This way, if I should die in here, I would be representing San Jo, Northern California to the fullest. Then I got to talk to Gordy. "Tell me that you love me, baby, and that you will pray for me, my love."

Man oh man, what a filthy jailhouse in LA; the roaches were having their little spreads. Talk about a dirty, dirty place to do your time. When I was in the San Jo jailhouse doing my time, I never saw one little roach. I chilled out by myself for a minute and kept looking at all the writing in the cell, then I saw HOPPER in big letters. That was what they used to call my dead little brother. When I had seen that name, I did not feel so all alone; I felt like my dead little brother was watching over me, like an angel or something. Then all the prison time and my jail time started to kick in. This became very useful in my situation—in a good way. So I began to notice the danger from a distance. *Are you friend or foe?* Well, I got to talking to this other inmate; he was White. We started to talk about the Bible and said a little prayer that God would see both of us through this nightmare. Then I started to do my workout, and I felt much stronger after seeing HOPPER on the wall. I did my fourteen sets. That made me happy, and I did not feel so sad. I did my northern Aztec workout, and I was feeling Aztec and acting Aztec. So now I was holding my ground but still keeping low-key at the same time. I was letting these other inmates know that I got down for mine. Just another way of saying "I do work out, and I got some wind, and I'm preparing for battle at the drop of a dime—any place and anytime." See, it was all way different behind enemy lines. They didn't ask you if you gangbanged. They didn't even ask you your name anymore. It was "Where are you from, and what set do you represent?" There was no respect for you or what you were about. See, I'd seen this in the joint and in the jailhouse, so that was a blessing to me—to be aware of my surroundings. The thing was that I was from up north, period; that was all to the bad being in a southern jail. I still, to this day, wonder why I did not just cry and break down or something. Well, I was lucky that I stayed strong in my time of weakness. I was just trying to keep my self-composure, minding my own business, and still talking to this Christian bro.

Now the day was almost over, and we had eaten our bean burritos. Then we watched the baseball game, the playoffs, and it was bedtime. I really don't even know how I could sleep, but I did—with one eye open. Well, the next day was Monday, and it was a holiday

(Labor Day), so there was no court. Then we got some more burritos for our breakfast; I did get my eat on. I was still doing my workout in the corner of the cell. Hey, and this time was just passing by, thank God. I still got this Christian brother in my cell, so we kept saying our prayers. "Thank you, God, for letting me see my brother's name on the wall. It felt to be a small miracle—really, a big miracle. Hopper, booyah, here's another set just for you, my baby brother. Keep me strong all day long, for I know that when they let me out for court, I'm a marked man—all eyes on me the enemy, the man from up north." I knew that the shit was gonna kick off in a bad way, baby. I just didn't know when, but it was gonna happen.

The next day passed, and it was Tuesday, and I still didn't hear my name for court. So then I called my work and told them that I was in jail, but not in San Jo. I said that I was in the LA jail. I asked them to say a prayer for me and to tell the other brothers I worked with to say a prayer too. I said that I was in a bad spot and that I got busted for something that was out of my hands. I still was just keeping the faith and saying my prayers; I did my workout in the cell. Then the next day, they did call my name, and I walked out of the cell and got handcuffed to another inmate. He had *sur 13* on his hand; he was a lowrider *vato*. We did not talk too much; he just wanted to see the judge. He had the southern trademark, and I had the northern trademark. Mine was under my shirt, on my stomach—*San Jo, Northern Cali*. Then they put us on the bus taking us to the courthouse. When we got there, they took us off the bus and took off the handcuffs. Now we were in the tunnels and in holding tanks. There was about thirty in the tank I was in; I was just checking all these hope-to-die southerners, tattoos, LA.

These were some ride-or-die southern warriors; remember, I still got my Nike's. So I sat down in my little corner, checking these hard-core lowriders *vatos*. I was still keeping low-key, not trying to call any attention to myself. Well, about ten minutes later, this one *vato* hit me up and asked me what was up with my Nike's. Then he told me to give them to him or they would give them to the Blacks. So I got up from standing and told him that I was from up north and didn't know how they ran this jailhouse. Then I gave up my Nike's, and he gave me his shower shoes and went back to his seat without fronting me off to his southern homies. Well, he told me that it was one big family, the Latinos. Then he hit up this border brother who had some Nike's too, and he was looking at me with tears about to fall from his eyes. Then all of a sudden, they started to call out names for court. I just felt that the Aztec way was if you got caught by the other tribe, you should give them a gift out of good gesture; that was the way I felt about the Nike's. Well, they called his name; all I could see was my Nike's walking out the cell, plus they called out about twenty names. Now there was only about six other southerners in my tank. There was this one big southerner who was just showing off his size, and he had *sureno* on his stomach. For some reason, I had known that we would get them up and fight. So he came up to me and asked me where I was from. I said San Jose, then he went and talked with these young warriors at the other end of the tank. They called him Peanut; I had been keeping my eye on him all along. Then he came at me again. "Hey, brother, where you from?" I said San Jose. Well, I was sitting on the bench, then he cracked me two times. Then I got up and cracked him back and started to get him off me, and I was landing some good shots of my own. Now he was backing up, and I kept cracking him, then you could hear some keys, and he saw the guard and put down his hands, and I came all the way back and cracked him and dropped him. San Jo Shark, boy.

Then the guard asked why we were fighting, and I picked up my shirt. I told him that we were fighting because of *San Jo* on my stomach and that I was a northern Aztec warrior and I represented my hometown. I said we fought out of respect for where we were from. Then before they let me out the cell, I thanked the young southern warriors for letting us fight one-on-one. I popped my collar, then that guy Peanut said, "Why didn't you guys help me out?" I started to ball out laughing. The guard asked me if I wanted to go another round. I said that it didn't matter to me. "Hey, let me see who is running this here floor. My civil rights have been violated to the fullest." I showed them my paperwork. "Where's your squad leader?" Then they put me in a cell all by myself; finally, I talked to this Latino officer who was up on the gang warfare between the north and the south.

In about two hours, they set me free. They didn't even send me a rookie. This was a grown man's game. They kicked me out of that LA courthouse with two black eyes. What a blessing to me. Thank you, Lord. That fight was truly a blessing in disguise. So here I was walking in Downtown Los Angeles with just my slippers and my cutoffs, trying to get to the Greyhound bus station. I finally made it there and called Gordy's mom and told her that I just got out of jail and to send me some money so I could make it back to San Jose. My nightmare was finally over. They asked me how I had got out, so I told them, "From fighting with a southern boy, and they kicked me to the curb." Gordy's mom sent my money through Western Union, and I got it. Now I was back on track. I did not have any wallet or nothing, so my password was Chino ESSJ. After I got the money, I got something to eat and started talking to this one young man who was selling some Nike's for ten bucks, so I got them. Then I went and got my one-way ticket to San Jose and waited for the bus to leave. I got me a pack of smokes, put on my shoes, and was good to go.

All I was thinking about was how I had got set up for the fall. I sure felt like the fall guy by Gordy's brother and his people. Then I was so happy to get out of that hellhole. If I wanted to be forgiven, I had to learn how to forgive, not forget. Then I felt that those Los Angeles officers had set me up to get my ass kicked to the curb. You just don't put a northern man with all kinds of southern men, and that's a fact. They just didn't know any better, I guess. Who could I trust? Only the Lord. I was sure that those LA officers knew that my life was in their hands. Funny now, it seemed like it backfired on them all. For I still stood tall with my back against the wall. Then my bus was ready to leave; I hopped of the bus and got ghost. I told that southerner thanks and that I got to go back to San Jo. So now I was rolling back to my hometown, and all was going just fine—just got these two black eyes. Hey, a little gift from Peanut, my pal. Then those black eyes would be gone in about two weeks. Right when I got off the bus in San Jo, I kissed the ground. I said, "I do, San Jo, love you." I thanked the Lord up above for bringing me back safe and sound. Then I got on the transit bus to get to the house of Gordy's mom. I then knocked on the front door.

"Hey, Chino, what's up? Come inside. Whoa, look at those black eyes you got."

"No biggie. I say give me two weeks, and I will be as good as new."

Delia, Gordy's mom, said, "Here is your old gym bag that you left me."

"Hey, Delia, can I take me a long-overdue shower?"

"Go ahead."

"Cool. I'm all stinky, like a lost dog or something."

She laughed and gave me a hug.

That shower was priceless, so fresh and so clean. Then I went into my gym bag. I had two joints in there and got my smoke on to kill the pain. My body was still feeling sore. Then Delia made me something for breakfast—good home cooking, yes. I wanted to live it out and not stress it out. I was feeling a lot better now, kinda back on track. Then I got Gordy's little brother blowing me up in a good gangster way. "Hey, you know Chino, my brother-in-law, got busy with a scrap in the LA jailhouse and beat him down." Now my reputation preceded me. "Hey, ain't you Chino, who got busted in LA and walked the main line then boxed for us northern brothers?" That put me on gangster status and moved up in respect. Then I called Gordy and let her know that I was out of that hellhole. I talked to Destiny; she told me that she was happy that they let me out of that LA jailhouse.

"See, mija, if you really pray and keep the faith, the Lord will hear you." Well, there was a story in the Bible from the book of Judges. This one mighty warrior named Jephthah vowed to the Lord and said, "If thou shalt deliver the children of Ammon into my hands, and I am victorious, then it shall be that whatever comes out from the doors of my house to meet me when I return in peace from the children of Ammon, it will surely be the Lord's, and I will offer it up for a burnt offering." So Jephthah went to war and had a great slaughter and won. Then when Jephthah got home, behold, his daughter came out to meet him with timbrels and dances, and she was his only child. Beside her, he had neither son nor daughter. "Alas, my daughter. Thou hast brought me very low, and thou art one of them that trouble me. For I have opened my mouth unto the Lord and cannot go back."

Then she said to her father, "If thou hast opened your mouth unto the Lord, do to me according to that which hath proceeded out of thy mouth. For as much as the Lord hath taken vengeance for thee of thine enemies." All his daughter wanted was her father. Then she said to her father, "Let this thing be done for me. Let me alone for two months, that I may go up and down the mountains and bewail my virginity." After the two months that she returned to her father, who did which he had vowed, and she knew no man. I was touched by this story; it reminded me of being in that LA jail. Then I came out with the Lord's blessing. Hey, maybe the Lord heard Destiny when she was praying for her father and honored both our prayers. I thanked the Lord for his blessings.

Well, it was time to get my ass back to work at Glassforms. I took the bus to get there; about two thirty, I left the house of Gordy's mom to give me time to catch the next bus. I didn't want to be late. It sure felt good to be back in San Jo and still have my job. When I had called my job from the LA jail and asked them to pray for me, they said that they would. "May our Lord bless you for that, and tell all my brothers at work that I send my love and utmost respect."

"Will do this for you, William. Now you take care of yourself."

Hey, this way, my job knew that I was not playing when I missed work and that I was in the Twin Towers in LA jailhouse. So if I did not make it back, it was no secret. So when I showed up for work, everybody was all around me. "Hey, William, we was praying for you, brother. We are glad to see you even with them two black eyes." I told them that I worked for these black eyes, 15,000 for each one. They all gave me long respect and some gangster hugs. I told them if they believed in miracles, well, I was that miracle, baby boy, booyah. "What's up, you northern Aztec warrior you?" Then I didn't hate all this mad respect that I was getting; it felt real good.

My friend Sly came and sat down next to me. "Wat the heck happened, brother?"

So I ran down the story. "I was going to see Gordy and Destiny in Arizona and got pulled over, and the van was stolen, but I had not known nothing about that. Then I had to slang them with the biggest southerner in the tank. First, he broke me off, then I had to break him off too till he fell to the ground."

Sly told me, "You a badass brother from our hometown, San Jo, represent." So then he gave me a lightweight job because he knew that I was still hurting; nobody had a problem with that—really out of respect for what I had to go through. Then I showed them my paperwork, and they knew that I did represent Northern California and San Jo in a major way. "Northern gang, you put your life on the line, William. Love you for that. Hey, whatever you need, we got you."

I and what I did represented till death San Jo, my city of no pity, do-or-die on mine. We had some northern Aztec Warriors from Pelican Bay who gave me my due respect. They told me if I needed anything or if anybody messed with me, they got my back. "We shall be there for you, Chino."

I felt that I was untouchable; I had a status that was the highest in loyalty and the utmost respect and honor. "Thanks, that's good to know, *pero* it's all good, brothers. I'm just happy to be back here in San Jo with my brothers at work. Amen."

Then in about two weeks, my black eyes went away. Just a little healing time, and I was back, looking good once again. Hey, all I really wanted to do was to visit my Destiny and Gordy. It was too bad; I wanted Gordy's mother and her mother, Delia (Gordy's grandma), with our little Destiny all together in one place before it was too late. See, Gordy's grandma was very old, and her time might come at any minute. Things did not go as planned. We had got sidetracked when I got arrested in LA. That was when it went all bad. That was five days and nights of madness, one big nightmare that I was blessed to get out of by the grace of our Lord. Well, that was all in the past, so next time I'd go visit, I would take the Greyhound or catch Southwest Airlines. Now I was saving my little cash for my next trip to Arizona. No, I was not even crazy—just felt I wanted to finish what I had started. Then I still kept talking to Gordy and told her that I still wanted to go and visit. She told me, "Just be careful."

"I will, baby doll. All about that safe Greyhound."

Gordy told me, "When you are ready, I will be waiting for you."

It seemed like our love affair had grown strong for what had happened to me in LA. Hey, maybe now she felt that I put my life on the line just to come and visit her and Destiny. It was like Gordy was my little sexy reward for me going to jail and getting those two black eyes. Well, we were still talking on the phone. Then one night at work, a coworker said, "Hey, Chino, your lady wants you on the phone."

"What's up, my love?"

Then she said, "Just been thinking of you, Chino."

"Is that right, Gordy?"

Then Gordy told me, "Talk sexy to me, daddy."

I said, "Oh, you want some of that long-distance phone sex?"

She said, "Why, yes."

I told her, "Just wait till I get off work and get back to the house.

"Okay, daddy."

I could not wait to get home and talk sexy to Gordy till I got there in person. "Hey, Gordy, I'm home and ready to talk nasty to you, and you can talk dirty to me."

She said, "What are you gonna do to me when you see me?"

"First, I'm gonna give you a good long licking, get you all naked, put you in a sexy outfit, and play with your sexy, silky legs."

Well, we talked for about fifteen minutes, and she told me that she came, and it felt like I was right there making love to her. Gordy was grateful to me and told me that would hold her till I got there in person. I told her to give me two more weeks and I'd be right over there. Then we said good night, and she blew me some kisses over the phone. I told her to tell Julian and Destiny that I would be over in about two more weeks.

The next day, I got back to work, and they gave me Employee of the Month and $100, which was right on time. I was still getting the engine rebuilt and needed some more money for my trip back to visit Destiny. I was still working swing shift, and everything on my machine was running good. I went to lunch and ate with my home-boys. We ordered a couple of pizzas and had a spread. We listened to some music and got our smoke on before getting back to work. I talked to Sly about giving me a ride after work. "No problem." On the way to my house, we were listening to the radio, and this one song played: "Your Body All Over My Body."

"What the heck? Did you hear that, bro? That song will get Gordy in the mood, that's for sure."

I was ready to go back to Arizona. I got my stuff together and told my dad to give me a ride to the bus station. I was playing it safe this time. I bought my round-trip ticket for $120 and put my stuff on the bus. Cool. I did miss Gordy and Destiny so much; I couldn't wait to get there.

I finally got there to Arizona with my little bit of stuff and called Gordy. "Hey, babe, come and pick me up."

Then she told me, "Is this for real?"

"Just come and get me here at the bus station. I will be waiting for you."

Then Gordy said, "Let me get Julian and Destiny ready."

Gordy got there in about ten minutes, yes. When she got there, I couldn't wait to hold her and give her a big, long kiss. Then when I saw my other two angels, I gave them hugs and kisses. Then I told Gordy, "Come here again, you sexy thing." Then I saw some tears coming from Gordy's eyes, and she told me how happy she was that they didn't kill me when I was in that Los Angeles jail. I wiped her tears away, and we went to grandma's house. We got some Coronas and some snacks for the kids. Soon as we got to her house, we made a toast and salute to all the fallen northern Aztec Warriors who were do-or-die and who represented to the death, shaw, booyah.

"Now come here, you sexy baby doll." We went into the room, and I put my stuff away.

Then Gordy said, "Lock the door." She puts on her sexy little teddy bear outfit, and I got into my boxers and got my camera ready to take some photos of Gordy, looking all sexy now. Then after the photos, she came to bed and let me mount her from behind till I finally busted one. She said, "How do you want it? How does it feel?" And I was as hard as steel. So we got our little freak on and cleaned up. We came back out of the room and started chilling like a northern villain. I was playing with my Julian and my little Destiny, taking some more photos of them. Destiny had such a pretty smile. Then we ate some dinner and drank some more brew till it was about bedtime. So I put the children to sleep. Then Gordy and I went to the bedroom and finished just what we started. She was so horny now, and so was I. So now she put on her sexy bra and panties, and we started to make out. She was hot and juicy, all nice and wet in her kitty cat and all primed and ready to go. I was lying on my back, and she started to mount me, taking all my hard loving, whoa.

Then Gordy was making all these sexy moans, making me feel like a northern Aztec king under the sheets till a sound of ecstasy was heard in the room. Then she put her head on my chest, kissing me at the same time. She was telling me, "What would I do if something happened to you. You're my baby's daddy and my daddy too." Then I told her that she had kept me strong and proud when I was in that LA jail. Gordy told me that I made her feel like a true Azteca queen. "Only when I'm with you, Chino." She knew all the right words to say to me. While I was trying to say all the right words to her at the same time. I felt that we were truly made for each other in God's eyes.

"Now lay your pretty face on my chest, and let's get some rest."

We fell asleep in each other's arms. I thanked the Lord for all his beautiful blessings. I felt now I had come full circle with that bad LA experience. I learned from my mistakes; you might learn from mine.

I woke up the next morning with Gordy's warm, sexy body right next to mine. Then I woke her up with some more hard loving, and she did not mind. She said, "Take me, baby. I'm all yours."

"That's what I'm talking about, lover. Now open up them sexy thighs and let me inside them sugar walls." I smelled fire and smoke down there in the kitty cat. Meow meow. Then let me give her some warm milk.

"Um, yum yum. Give me some."

Then I got Gordy mounted to the bed, and she was loving it. I finally got mine, and she got hers. Yeah, it was relief of that sexual tension—just making up for all that lost time. Gordy's kitty cat was purring after I was done with her. It was like having my own *Playboy* centerfold in a blessed way. Then I took some more snapshots of

Gordy; she was a little bashful at first. Then she was a natural, posing in all kinds of sexy positions. "Hey, Jennifer Lopez has got nothing on you, my darling. You look like a movie star, and you are mine oh mine." I had never been to heaven; instead, I spent the night with Gordy, the next best thing—if you know what I mean, booyah.

Now we got up from our lovemaking and washed up. We started to get our breakfast ready. I made me some coffee and helped out my Gordy with cooking the *papas* and bacon. Then I woke up Julian and Destiny. "Get up, you lazy little rascals. Go and wash up, Destiny. Then you too, Julian, wash your face and brush your teeth. Your mom is almost done with our breakfast. Are you hungry?"

"Yes."

Gordy was my sexy little chef, whom I loved the best. We all got our eat on, and Gordy and I cleaned up the mess and let Destiny and Julian outside to play. So Destiny was riding her bike, and Julian's bike had a flat tire. Then we walked to the corner store and got some patches, and I fixed the flat and put in some air, and Julian was good to go. "Hey, Chino, watch me do some tricks on my bike." So I watched him do his stuff; Gordy was looking from the inside window. Julian told Gordy, "Look, Mom, Chino fixed my bike, so I can ride with my friends." I came inside to clean myself up and put the tools away.

It was about lunchtime now, and Gordy said "Let's go to the room" and locked the door. "Thank you for fixing my son's bike. Now you can make love to me some more. Get yours, daddy. How do you want me?"

I peeled off her sexy little red panties and mounted her from behind, pulling her hair from the back; and she felt oh so tight, like a hand in glove, perfect, till I came all inside of her. "Whoa, Gordy, that was good loving baby." I cleaned up and left the room first, then Gordy came out. "Where's my little Destiny?" I went outside to play with her, got my camera, and took some photos of her on her bike then some of Julian on his bike. Then we took some of all of us together. All good things come to those who wait. Hey, and I waited for this to be real. So I must thank our Lord once again for bringing us all together once again. My little visit was for only three days and three nights, so all that I could do was make the best of this time. Better than nothing was all I got to say. So we started to celebrate our good fortune. We started drinking some Coronas and having a good time, playing with Destiny.

Then I got little Destiny sitting on my lap and Julian right at my side trying to make the best of it. Destiny and Julian were telling me that they didn't want me to go back. "I know, my mija, but Daddy has to go to work and make some money. I don't like it, but what can I do?" I told Destiny, "Let's just enjoy this time that we have now, deal, my daughter?"

She said "Okay, Daddy" and gave me a kiss. It was starting to get late, and Destiny told me that she was getting sleepy. So I got her ready for bed, took her inside, and tucked her in. Then we said our prayers, and she fell asleep. I kissed her on the cheek. I said, "Sleep with the angels, my Destiny. My one and only daughter, your daddy loves you forevermore." Then I went back outside and drank another Corona with Gordy and her tia Blanca. We were listening to some tight oldies, and I was enjoying Gordy's nice kisses, and she was close to me. Now it was about midnight, so I got ready to go to sleep and gave Gordy a good night kiss. Her tia told me, "Are you gonna get your beauty sleep?"

"Yeah, if that's what you call it." Then I told her, "Have a good one, Tia."

So I was fast asleep in Gordy's bed, then all of a sudden, Gordy woke me up. Then she was like a tiger, and she put her hot kitty cat all up in my mouth, and I started licking her. Then she was mounting me, and I sure didn't hate it, and I was playing with her soft breast till she was about to come in my mouth, making her sexy moans. "Right there, daddy. Oh, baby." So now it was my turn to mount her, and I put her on top of me and grabbed her firm breast, and she was loving it—sexy. Then I finally busted one, and Gordy said, "I'm not done with you, big daddy." So we chilled out while I reloaded. We got some sexy oldies playing in the background. Then Gordy said, "Are you ready for some more hot loving?"

"Why, yes, I am, my lover." Then I hit her from the side, beating up this hot, juicy loving till I busted another one. It was good to be in that northern Aztec warrior shape; it all paid off. I was doing my push-ups all this time to feel sexy to Gordy so that when our bodies would finally meet, she would feel my hard body.

We made love till the sun came out. "You was hungry for me, Gordy."

"You know that I'm always hungry for you, my baby's daddy."

Now both of us were tuckered out from all that lovemaking, so we fell asleep. I made the most of this time that I had with Gordy, Destiny, and Julian. We slept late the next morning and got our beauty sleep. I woke up about eleven and let Gordy sleep till about one in the afternoon. Then when Gordy woke up, I told her, "Hey, my love, I wore you out, and you wore me out too—in a loving way." I saw that sexy smile of hers that drove me just crazy. I was thinking that this would be my last night here and started to feel sad. Well, I shook it off and took it in stride and stayed in a good mood. I played with Destiny and Julian outside, playing on their bikes. Even Gordy was feeling sad; she knew that I would be taking off once again. "Hey, babe, come on now. We had a good time. Let's just make the best of the time that we have left." We had a small barbecue and drank some Coronas and got our grub on.

The time was passing by so fast, then it was starting to be about dinnertime. My bus was leaving at about eight that night, so I got to start getting ready to go. I told myself it was all good; I got to visit my daughter and my son then got some good loving with a smile from my lover, Gordy. Yeah, yeah, my life was so sweet and even just for a little while. So I was in the room getting my stuff ready when Gordy came in and locked the door. Then she got all naked. "Let me give some for the road, my lover." Then I got under the sheets, and we shared some more lovemaking before I went.

"Tell me that you love me."

"Chino, you know that I love you, daddy. Take all this hot kitty cat till we can be together again."

I couldn't get enough of Gordy, then I busted one, and we cleaned up. It was that time. "Let's get this over with and take me to the bus station." I put my stuff in the car, and off we went. Once we got there, I got my stuff ready; and Gordy, Destiny, Julian, and

I said our goodbyes with tears coming from our eyes. I'd miss those precious kisses.

Well, I got back to San Jose once again. That was home base for me, and I unpacked all my goodies. Then I did a check on the Monte Carlo, and she was all most done. I got back to work. Well, in about two weeks, Gordy called me to let me know that she had found a new man. That broke my heart, but what could I do? Just be thankful for all our precious moments and our beautiful daughter, Destiny. Who said that you get to live happy ever after? All you can do is make the best out of this situation.

So this is where my story will end. My little Destiny is now seventeen years young and still is pure and is doing well in school. I still am a proud father. I just wanted to share this story with the rest of the world. Hey, maybe my story might help some of the young northern Aztec warriors out when they need a story to read some of the changes in this life we lead. Well, God bless and take care.

Here is a poem in honor of my little brother:

> For you tell me that I must perish
> Like the flowers that I cherish
> Nothing remaining of my name
> Nothing remembered of my fame
> For the gardens I planted are still young
> And the songs I sang
> Shall still be sung.

This was written by an Aztec prince of Texcoco, Huexotzin, in California (1484).

Chino Ruiz
EIIJ 14

For I thank you, Lord,
For giving me something to do
Instead of being bored
In my lonely room.
Peace of mind
Is so hard to find.
We must think
Before we speak.
Where the strong
Prey upon the weak,
San Jo ★ gangster,
Make a toast and drink.
        Amen.
        Chino Ruiz

Chino Destiny #96

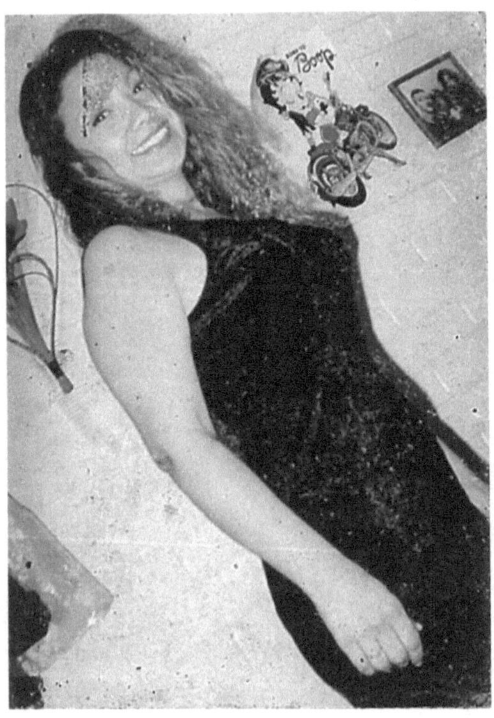

Gordy #97 My Lady

Lit Hopper. Before He died 1980

Gordy #97 Babydoll ★

My Jennifer Lopez

About the Author

This story is about my troubles, after my little brother was murdered. At only fourteen years young. The changes that I put myself through. Then how I have become a better and wiser man, Amen.